New Hampshire
War Monuments

New Hampshire War Monuments
The Stories Behind the Stones

Kathleen D. Bailey and Sheila R. Bailey
Foreword by Senator Maggie Hassan

THE
History
PRESS

Published by The History Press
Charleston, SC
www.historypress.com

Copyright © 2022 by Kathleen Bailey and Sheila Rose Bailey
All rights reserved

First published 2022

Manufactured in the United States

ISBN 9781467151184

Library of Congress Control Number: 2022936632

To the Five Manchester Guardsmen.

Contents

Foreword: War Monuments of New Hampshire:
The Stories Behind the Stones, by Senator Maggie Hassan   9
Acknowledgements   11
Introduction: War Monuments   15
A Note to Readers   19

1. The Revolution, the French and Indian War and
   the War of 1812   21
2. A House Restored: The Civil War   45
3. Over There and Over Here: The First World War   77
4. Paying the Price: The Second World War   113
5. The Shape of Things to Come: The Korean War   138
6. My Brother's Keeper?: The Vietnam War   151
7. A New Reality: Iraq and Afghanistan   167
8. A Place to Reflect: The Cathedral of the Pines   183

Appendix: The Merci Boxcar, the Marine Memorial,
   the Submarine Memorials at the Albacore, the Veterans
   Cemetery, the Wright Museum, the War Dog
   Memorial, Manchester's Squares and the Sculptors   191
The Last Word   211
Notes   215
About the Authors   221

Foreword

War Monuments of New Hampshire

The Stories Behind the Stones

In the fall of 2021, when Kathleen Bailey first reached out to me about her book, *New Hampshire War Monuments: The Stories Behind the Stones*, I was working with my colleagues in the Senate on a bipartisan bill to build a war memorial on the National Mall in Washington, D.C., honoring those who served in the Global War on Terrorism and their families. We have now passed into law our legislation to ensure that this memorial can be built on the National Mall, and it will serve as a place to gather, reflect and honor those who have given their lives for our country.

The story of building the National Mall's Global War on Terrorism Memorial echoes those of our memorials in New Hampshire, with veterans and their families, civilians and lawmakers coming together to create sacred places for generations of Americans to honor those who have who fought, led and, in many cases, died, all to keep Americans safe, secure and free.

New Hampshire has a long, proud legacy of military service that has shaped the history of the United States of America from the Revolutionary War to today. Throughout our state's history, brave men and women have put on their uniforms and traveled far from home, knowing the risks in front of them. But beyond those risks, these individuals knew that their missions were paramount to our freedom and our democracy.

The reverence that we carry for these heroes and the sacrifices that they have made on behalf of each and every one of us must be everlasting, informing every generation of Americans. It started, of course, with our reverence for our founders, who pledged in the Declaration of

Independence, "our lives, our fortunes and our sacred honor." The question for every generation of Americans since then has been whether we have done the work necessary to make our country ever worthy of those original sacrifices—and the service and sacrifices of all who have served, some making the ultimate sacrifice, to keep freedom's flame alive.

It is in that spirit that towns and cities throughout New Hampshire have erected monuments to honor our heroes. In every corner of our state, you will find tributes of all shapes and sizes—in town squares, parks and schools and in solemn locations like our magnificent and peaceful Veterans' Cemetery. Each of these memorials serve an important purpose: they help us remember our fallen and ensure that they are never forgotten. Behind each of these monuments are stories of brave individuals who gave everything—their very being—in the name of freedom. And at their root is a deep, often instinctive, understanding of why the idea of a free, self-governing people is worth fighting for.

New Hampshire War Monuments: The Stories Behind the Stones helps share many of those stories. As you read, you'll learn more about monuments across the Granite State and learn about some of the lives and legacies central to New Hampshire's and America's history.

I hope that by reading this book, you will develop a greater appreciation for these sacrifices and recognize the role that we all play in keeping the memory of our fallen heroes and what they fought for alive. I also hope that as you view these beautiful photographs and learn about these heroic stories, you are inspired to visit some of New Hampshire's war monuments and take time to reflect yourself.

Senator Maggie Hassan, D-NH
January 2022

Acknowledgements

*T*his was a project with many moving parts, and I could not have done it without help. Some researched their family archives. Some gave me permission to use a quote or a photograph. Others uncovered painful memories in order to show my readers how it really was. The following people deserve my thanks.

The Revolution, the French and Indian War and the War of 1812:

- Jane Stephenson, Plainfield Historical Society, for information and photographs on Derrick Oxford.
- *Journal of the American Revolution*, for permission to quote Kieran O'Keefe (September 2019).

The Civil War:

- George Morrison, author and Civil War specialist, general background information.
- *Yankee* magazine for permission to quote Castle Freeman (May 2015).
- Chicago Public Radio for permission to quote from "10 Monuments that Changed America."
- Warren Huse, author, for permission to use photographs of the Veterans' Association compound.

- JoAnn Tebbetts, for permission to use material on Loammi Bean.
- Chris Pratt and the Town of Sullivan.
- Bill Mulcahy and the Town of Washington.

The First World War:

- Virginia Drye, Plainfield Historical Society, for providing information and photographs of Harry Thrasher.
- St. Paul's School/Andrew Seamans for permission to use a photograph of the Daniel Chester French sculpture.

The Second World War:

- John Clayton, Manchester Historic Association, for providing information on Rene Gagnon.
- *New Hampshire Union Leader*, for permission to use a quote (October 21, 2019).
- The Milford Historical Society, for permission to use a photograph of the Thirteen Trees.
- Patrick Hummel, from Mount Washington, for permission to use a photograph of the Tenth Mountain Division plaque.

The Korean Conflict:

- Maurice Mailhot of Berlin for permission to use photographs and reminiscences.
- John S. "Jack" Barnes of Raymond for permission to use his reminiscences.
- The Concord, New Hampshire Historical Society.
- The Library of Congress, Historic American Engineering Record.
- Jim Spain of Concord for providing information on the Korea Bridge.
- Hillsborough County Genealogy, for providing material on Roger Cote.

The Vietnam War:

- *New Hampshire Union Leader* for permission to use a quote (August 24, 2019, and August 26, 1969).

- Celine M. Therrien for permission to use reminiscences of the Five Guardsmen.
- The Chase-Bouchard family for permission to use reminiscences and a photograph of William Fraser.
- Hillsborough County Genealogy for providing background material on Winston Taggart and the Five Guardsmen.
- The U.S. Department of Veterans Affairs for providing studies on Vietnam War veterans.

Iraq and Afghanistan:

- Mrs. Nicole Dicenzo for permission to use memories and photographs of Douglas DiCenzo.
- Floyd Burlock for permission to use reminiscences and photographs of Randy Rosenberg.
- Mrs. Natalie Healy for permission to use memories of Dan Healy.

Appendix A:

- Tony Travia for hosting an afternoon at the Merci Boxcar.
- Betty Moore and the Hampton Historical Society for providing information and photographs of the Marine Memorial.
- Gretchen Ziegler for providing material on the Cathedral of the Pines.
- The Wright Museum for permission to use photography exhibits.

The Last Word:

- Jim Pope of Brookline for permission to use photographs and information on the *Pillars of Freedom*.

Miscellaneous help and advice:

- Richard Marsh, photographer.
- Matthew Thomas, historian.
- George Morrison, Civil War specialist.

Additional thanks to:

- Senator Maggie Hassan and her staff for the foreword.
- My editor Mike Kinsella.
- My daughter and coauthor, Sheila R. Bailey.
- My daughter Autumn Kent for providing endless tech support.
- My husband, David, for his unwavering support in all of my writing endeavors.
- And the dozens of historical societies, Veterans of Foreign Wars (VFWs) and American Legions that provided information for this project. There are too many to list.

Kathleen D. Bailey (February 2022)

Introduction

War Monuments

I grew up in the '50s in the home of two avid sightseers. While my parents weren't much for traveling outside of New England, they loved to visit spots around the Northeast. We didn't see the "U.S.A. in a Chevrolet," but we cruised New Hampshire in a Nash Rambler. The low gas prices and the Eisenhower Interstate Highway System streamlined travel, and we took to the road.

My father had a particular curiosity, and we frequently stopped to read the inscriptions on moss-covered plaques and granite columns. Everything had a story, especially the monuments to those who had served in the U.S. Armed Forces. My father served in World War II, and as with other veterans of that era, the bitter war in Europe was still a living thing to him. Our people had won, but they knew the cost. It was all around them. And the veterans knew the story behind each obelisk.

I thought of my father when, after half a lifetime, I revisited the *Buddies Monument* in Jaffrey. The World War I monument is simple but stunning, a doughboy carrying his dead comrade off the field. I delved into its history and learned that there's a love story at its core: a Danish sculptor had donated his time and talent to the town where his late wife had spent her summers. But there was more than one love story in the *Buddies Monument*: the platonic love between the two soldiers, the romantic love that sent Viggo Brandt-Erichsen across the ocean and the love of freedom that propelled young men to go to Europe.

This story sparked my curiosity about New Hampshire's memorials, monuments and other tributes to those who served. I learned that other famous sculptors, including Daniel Chester French, put their skills to work to honor war casualties (like Exeter's Gale Park statue). I learned the background of Concord's Memorial Arch and Exeter's public library, both memorials to the War Between the States. I learned the history of the ubiquitous "Single Soldiers" found on town commons from Coos County to the Massachusetts border. And as I talked to veterans and survivors from around the state, I knew I had a book.

Two of the state's smaller towns share the distinction—and a friendly rivalry—of having the first war monuments in the state. According to Washington town historian Bill Mulcahy, the town began planning a monument to its Civil War casualties in late 1865. The cost, with all funds provided by public donation, was $2,000 (or $37,500 at the time of this book's publication). Former New Hampshire governor Frederick Smyth dedicated the obelisk on September 7, 1867. According to Mulcahy, Washington sent fifty-three men to fight in the War Between the States. Of these men, twelve did not return, and they are commemorated on the monument. Three were killed in action, and nine died from disease. The monument is located on the town common, along with the 1787 Meetinghouse, now the town hall; the 1840 Congregational Church; and the 1887 Central Schoolhouse. "These," Mulcahy said, "make Washington's beautiful common arguably the most photographed in New Hampshire."

But Sullivan may have chipped away at Washington's glory. Town archivist Chris Pratt says that his town was the first to raise and dedicate a monument in New Hampshire. The story of the Sullivan Soldiers' Monument began well before the Civil War, and as with many small-town achievements, it stemmed from a group of determined women. In 1840, women from the Sullivan Congregational Church formed the Sullivan Female Circle of Industry. When the war broke out, they organized the Sullivan Soldiers' Aid Society, providing aid and comfort to Union soldiers with everything from knitted socks to rolled bandages. When the war ended, they directed their energy toward raising funds for a monument to the Sullivan soldiers who had died during the war. They raised $300 on their own and another $500 from subscriptions around town. The total amount raised was $800, $15,000 in today's currency. Hubert Brennan of Keene, an Irish immigrant and owner of the Peterborough Marble and Granite Works, designed and produced the tribute. Sullivan dedicated its memorial on July 4, 1867, three months before the Washington monument was dedicated.

While the towns and often the state continue to remember those who have been lost, the complexion of those monuments has changed over three hundred years. Before the Civil War, the few memorials erected showcased victory and power. The Civil War, which no one really won, ushered in the image of the brooding "Single Soldier" preserving the Union—but at a cost. The Civil War and World War I also brought elaborate and emotional concepts into fashion, including allegorical figures, such as the Angel of Death and Death himself. World War II and the wars in Korea and Vietnam produced stark, pared-down remembrances as the country grappled with what these wars meant.

While young men and, more recently, women still have their names carved on an honor roll in the village square, their memories are just as likely to be kept alive through a recreational area, a town park, a swimming pool (Dan Healy of Exeter) or a road race or golf tournament (Dan Healy, the former, and Doug DiCenzo of Plymouth, the latter).

Today's monuments, memorials and tributes reflect the way these young men and women would want to be remembered. The recreational areas, parks and camp scholarships give the living a tangible way to remember the dead. And if the living pause before they hit a golf ball or while they're baiting a hook for a kid, it's OK. Is there a better way to be remembered?

Like their New England counterparts, the residents of New Hampshire often endure the "stoic Yankee" stereotype. But with the tenacity that dug farms out of rock, the residents of New Hampshire don't let go. The state's towns mourn deep, wide and long. Franklin put up a memorial to Vietnam casualty Jedh Barker, even though he had left the town at the age of six. And the clock stopped in Manchester one hot August day as Bishop Ernest J. Primeau and two thousand people came together at the city's small airport to accept the bodies of five National Guardsmen, all of whom were from the city's west side. They were all killed on the same day in Vietnam. Time slowed in the state's busiest city as Manchester welcomed its boys home for the last time.

This book is dedicated to the Five Guardsmen.

A Note to Readers

*I*n this book, we have dedicated two parts to each conflict: a chapter with narrative and a listing of other memorials to that war. The listings are organized by town and are centered on (1) that war and (2) the particular town that memorialized it. Some state memorials are included in the listings, especially in the Concord area.

The memorials to veterans of all wars were included in the Iraq/Afghanistan chapter, unless they specifically list different conflicts. For example, the Barrington All Wars Monument is dedicated to just that, while the Leander Cogswell Monument in Henniker carries plaques with names from major conflicts. Sometimes it's arbitrary, but we believe you'll find what you want.

We felt that the Cathedral of the Pines merited its own chapter. It grew out of a family's loss in World War II but has expanded to become much more. Appendix A lists and discusses venues that aren't necessarily town-specific or war-specific but speak to all the losses New Hampshire has sustained. The Marine Memorial isn't a Hampton thing; it's a New Hampshire thing. The Wright Museum in Wolfeboro isn't a Wolfeboro thing; it's a tribute to what everyone in New Hampshire did to win World War II. And the Veterans' Cemetery in Boscawen belongs to everyone.

The Revolution, the French and Indian War and the War of 1812

The flame of freedom burned no less brightly in the rocky, sparsely settled New Hampshire than it did in its larger neighbors or the rest of the thirteen original colonies. An incident in December 1774 drove the British from the Granite State, four months before the "shot heard round the world" in next-door Massachusetts. The incident had everything: Paul Revere, big guns and angry Yankees.

Fort William and Mary was located in New Castle, next door to Portsmouth and at the mouth of the Piscataqua River. It housed not only a supply of arms and powder for the King's regiments but also munitions for the fledgling Colonial militia. More than one hundred barrels of gunpowder were stored at the fort, along with sixteen cannons. On December 12, 1774, the Portsmouth Committee of Correspondence received a message from the Marblehead, Massachusetts Committee warning them that General Thomas Gage had issued an order prohibiting the Colonials from amassing weapons. After an incident in September in Massachusetts, it seemed likely that Gage was again going after supplies of Colonial munitions. At least one Royal Navy ship was headed for Portsmouth.

But Paul Revere could ride faster than the ship could sail, and he galloped the sixty-six miles northward in a snowstorm to warn the Portsmouth Patriots. With this intelligence, John Langdon and a group of about fifty men headed for New Castle in a gundalow. Word spread, and within twenty-four hours, they were joined by other Portsmouth residents and others from New Castle, Rye and Kittery, Maine. Over several days, they stormed the fort,

WILLIAM & MARY RAIDS

Dec. 14-15, 1774, several hundred men overpowered the small British garrison at Castle William & Mary, now Fort Constitution, New Castle, and removed quantities of military supplies. These raids, set off by Paul Revere's ride to Portsmouth on Dec. 13, were among the first overt acts of the American Revolution.

Fort William and Mary in New Castle, later renamed Fort Constitution, was the scene of an early effort by Colonials to preserve their munitions. The event was a prequel to the Battle of Lexington and Concord, with Paul Revere, big guns and fast horses. *Sheila Bailey.*

seized gunpowder and cannons and hauled down the British flag. Captain John Cochran was relieved of his duty at the fort, and Royal Governor John Wentworth and his family left Portsmouth for good shortly after.

The War for Independence began in April 1775, but by the time the Patriots made history at Lexington and Concord, New Hampshire had already taken its stand.

The men who would eventually call themselves Granite Staters enlisted in three regiments of the Continental army, fighting at the Battle of Bunker Hill, the Battle of Bennington, the Saratoga Campaign and the Battle of Rhode Island.

New Hampshire contributed to the Patriot cause in several ways—from teenage drummer boys to buck-stops-here leadership. General John Stark was already a hero after the French and Indian War and had "retired" to his Manchester farm. But he couldn't resist the call to arms or to freedom.

Stark, one of New Hampshire's most notable figures in two wars, is memorialized in bronze on the New Hampshire State House lawn. John Stark was born in Londonderry in 1728 and lived to see the new nation birthed. He fought and led in both the French and Indian War and the American Revolution. He first fought with Rogers' Rangers in the French and Indian War, attaining the rank of captain. After that war, Stark was married and worked a farm and mill near Manchester for the next sixteen years, but he could not resist the call to action after the Battle of Lexington. Appointed colonel of a regiment of New Hampshire Militia, he fought in several decisive battles, ignoring orders and turning the tide of a major

Stark is also memorialized in his hometown of Manchester with this statue at Stark Park. *Sheila Bailey.*

engagement. While facing a British and Hessian force that was going to Bennington, Vermont, to capture Colonial supplies, Stark famously told his men, "Tonight, the American flag floats over yonder hill, or Molly Stark sleeps a widow." Stark and his men won the Battle of Bennington, leading to General Burgoyne's surrender after the Battle of Saratoga on October 17, 1777, after which he was awarded the title major general. Molly got her husband back, and he died in 1822 at his farm.

New Hampshire recognized early on what it had in Stark, and the legislature began considering a memorial to him in 1885. But it took a fiery sermon from preacher Dr. William Mackergo Taylor, a guest speaker at Concord's South Church, to get things done. Taylor told the congregation, "I am not well enough informed of your affairs to know whether your state has erected a statue of General Stark, but it ought to if it has not."[1]

The next day, a chapter of the Sons of the American Revolution formed and appointed a committee to petition the legislature. A resolution passed on August 15, 1889, and was later signed in by the governor. The winning bid for the design came from Carl Conrads of the New England Granite Works of Hartford, Connecticut. Conrads, born in Germany, was a veteran of the War Between the States. His bid included the granite pedestal as well as the bronze statue. The statue was cast in bronze by the Ames Manufacturing Company of Chicopee, Massachusetts, with the granite pedestal cast by John A. Fox of Boston. It was dedicated on October 23, 1890.

Conrads later sculpted Stark in marble, and the second statue was installed in the U.S. Capitol's Statuary Hall in 1894.

John Stark is also memorialized in Stark Park in Manchester's North End on land from Stark's former farm. Richard Reccia of Massachusetts, a European-trained sculptor, received its commission. Philanthropist Charles Bartlett donated $40,000 for the project and the park. The statue was unveiled on September 12, 1848.

By the time of the American Revolution, Portsmouth was already a center of shipbuilding and provided the USS *Ranger* and the *America*, both captained by John Paul Jones, and the USS *Raleigh*. These ships were built on Badger's Island, halfway between Portsmouth and Kittery, Maine, in the Piscataqua River.

Jones twice lived briefly in Portsmouth, once in 1777, while the *Ranger* was being built, and once in 1781–82, while the *America* was being built. The 1758 home where he rented a room is now a museum maintained by the Portsmouth Historical Society.

Producing heroes didn't depend on a town's size. Andrew McClary, a tavern keeper and the town clerk for Epsom, distinguished himself in the French and Indian War, working as a scout and leading a company of soldiers in search of the Natives who massacred and took prisoners from the McCall family of Salisbury. Born in Ireland, McClary moved to Epsom with his family and helped operate a tavern, where issues surrounding the Revolution were thoroughly discussed. His tavern was a frequent stopping place for John Stark and other supporters of the cause.

McClary honed his fighting skills as a boxer and wrestler in his youth and put them to the test in the French and Indian War, in which he served alongside Robert Rogers as one of his famous rangers. But he shone the brightest in the Revolution.

McClary was instrumental in leading the effort to seize American gunpowder from Fort William and Mary in December 1774. After learning of the Battles of Lexington and Concord, he led local militia on the seventy-mile trek to Cambridge, Massachusetts, where he joined up with John Stark. Stark gave him the rank of captain, and on the eve of the Battle of Bunker Hill, McClary gained the rank of major.

Right: General John Stark, shown here at the New Hampshire State House, led the Battle of Bennington, which led to Burgoyne's surrender. *Sheila Bailey.*

Below: Andrew McClary of Epsom gave his life for his infant country at Bunker Hill. *Sheila Bailey.*

MAJOR ANDREW MCCLARY

Andrew McClary served in the famed Rogers Rangers. He participated in the December 1774 raids on the British Fort, William & Mary in New Castle, at which time powder and munitions were seized. Learning of the pending conflict at Bunker Hill while tilling his land just south of here he left his plow in the furrow in his haste to meet the challenge. McClary was named 2nd in command to Col. John Stark of the 1st N.H. Regiment. A British cannonball felled him as the battle ended, prompting the eulogy: "His sun went down at noon on the day that ushered in our nation's birth".

2008

Since General Joseph Warren chose to fight as a private, McClary was technically the highest-ranking soldier to die at Bunker Hill. He was killed as he attempted to cross Charlestown Neck to rejoin his regiment. A plaque honoring McClary can be seen at the complex on Route 4 housing the Epsom library and Old Meetinghouse.

Not every hero saw combat. Matthew Thornton, an Irish immigrant, studied medicine in Massachusetts and established a practice in Londonderry, New Hampshire. He served as a surgeon in the French and Indian War, tending the New Hampshire militia in an expedition to Fort Louisberg in 1745. But his biggest contribution to the emerging nation was political. He served in the New Hampshire Provincial Assembly, the Committee of Safety, as speaker of the House of Representatives and in the New Hampshire Senate. He drafted the plan of government for New Hampshire to become a state.

And Thornton wielded his pen as a signer of the Declaration of Independence in November 1776. His signature wasn't as flashy as John Hancock's, but it said what it needed to: New Hampshire was all in.

He is remembered by two elementary schools, Matthew Thornton in Londonderry and Thornton's Ferry in Merrimack. The northern town of Thornton is named for him. The house he occupied in Derry, then part of Londonderry, is in the National Register of Historic Places. He is also honored by a historical marker on Route 3 in Merrimack, and he was buried in the eponymous Thornton Cemetery on the same road.

George Morrison, a Civil War scholar living in Bow, wrote that before the War Between the States, America did not erect many monuments to the heroes of the Revolution. "The Bunker Hill monument, an obelisk, was an early one, but raising funds was tricky. The Washington Monument (another obelisk) had been begun before the Civil War, but with few funds, little 'altitude' had been achieved," Morrison wrote in an e-mail. "An obelisk monument to the late General Nathanael Greene—a Rhode Islander and one of Washington's favorites—was erected in Savannah, Georgia, and there was an equestrian George Washington in Richmond, Virginia."[2]

But most of the tributes to the Patriots came to be long after they were gone. Scholar Kieran O'Keefe wrote in the *Journal of the American Revolution*:

> *Until the mid-nineteenth century, there were relatively few memorials to the Revolution, and those that were built were generally dedicated to the leaders of the Revolution or men who had taken up arms. These monuments frequently accused the British of being cruel and dishonorable enemies. The*

Matthew Thornton served as a physician in the French and Indian War, but his real strength was in politics, and he signed the Declaration of Independence for New Hampshire. *Sheila Bailey*.

1890s to the 1930s saw the greatest surge in monument building, largely driven by recently formed lineage groups, such as the Daughters of the American Revolution.[3]

O'Keefe noted that women Patriots and foreign contributors, such as Casimir Pulaski, also got their due during this period.

The Pulaski Monument can be found in the center of Pulaski Park in downtown Manchester at the junction of Pine, Bridge, Union and High Streets. It honors Brigadier General Casimir Pulaski, a Polish immigrant often called the "father of the American cavalry." Pulaski was a trusted senior officer to General George Washington.

Pulaski died in 1779 due to injuries suffered in the Battle of Savannah.

His memorial is a tribute to another great movement in American history: beating the Depression. The statue was erected under the auspices of the Works Progress Administration (WPA) and was completed in 1938. The sculptor was Lucien Hippolyte Gosselin.[4]

Brigadier General Casimir Pulaski, the "father of the American cavalry," is memorialized with this Lucien Gosselin statue in the Manchester park that also bears his name. *Sheila Bailey*.

Like many Black contributors in American history, Black Patriots are finally getting their due. O'Keefe wrote, "After a period of relatively few monuments from the 1940s through the 1960s, there was another surge with the bicentennial in 1970s. In the years since, the greatest development has been the increased recognition of Black Patriot participation in the Revolution, with monuments erected across the country to honor their service."

The construction of the memorial to Derrick Oxford took generations to be completed.

Oxford was enslaved by William Gallup of Hartland, Vermont. He enlisted for three years from Plainfield and fought at the Battles of Ticonderoga and Saratoga. Due to the research of Plainfield Historical Society president Jane Stephenson, Oxford's grave was identified and marked with a military headstone in keeping with his service.

Stephenson first became aware of Oxford when another member of the historical society mentioned that there were two Black people buried

Derrick Oxford, enslaved by a Vermont man, fought in the Revolution. His service was largely unremembered and unmarked until the Plainfield Historical Society rededicated his grave and marked it with a new headstone in 2018. *Sheila Bailey*.

in the remote Coryville Cemetery. Stephenson recalls saying, "Show me," and these two words led to three years of research and a soldier finally getting his due.

Stephenson learned that "Derrick," an enslaved man, was brought north from Stonington, Connecticut, by his owner, William Gallup. Derrick was older, a father whose children were baptized in the Stonington Church, and he was probably married, according to Stephenson. That didn't keep Derrick's owner from making him enlist and pocketing the money.

Though Stephenson was never able to find an accurate birth or death date for Derrick, she patched together most of his story. In the Revolution, he served with a member of the Cutler family of Plainfield, and after the war, he returned and made his home with the Cutlers. Stephenson is not certain whether he was enslaved by then or free. But sometime during the war, he adopted the last name "Oxford."

Derrick was buried in the same cemetery as the Cutlers, though he was buried away from the general burial area with a rough slab of rock marking the site instead of a gravestone. Stephenson wanted him to have a proper stone with an engraving. "I 'harangued' the Veterans' Administration until they were willing to pay for it," she said with a smile.

Derrick Oxford's descendants join Revolutionary reenactors to dedicate the new stone on Oxford's grave. *Plainfield Historical Society.*

Stephenson wasn't done yet. An avid genealogist, she began to wonder if any of Derrick's progeny had survived. She found his descendant Bonita Johnson of New Haven, who was also an avid genealogist. Johnson rounded up some of the extended family, and they agreed to attend the dedication of the stone.

But Stephenson still wasn't done. She also managed to track down descendants of William Gallup.

The new gravestone was dedicated on May 19, 2018, when community members, along with members of the First New Hampshire Regiment reenactment group and descendants of Oxford and Gallup held a brief service at the Coryville Cemetery in Plainfield. Though there wasn't a big "Kumbaya" moment, according to Stephenson, the descendants of both families chatted briefly and cordially.

Despite these changes, there has also been some continuity in the Revolutionary memorials. The themes have largely remained the same since the late 1700s, with monuments consistently emphasizing the patriotism, unity and sacrifice of the now-Americans who fought for freedom.

Monuments or not, New Hampshire knew what it wanted. After the U.S. Constitution was written, New Hampshire was the ninth and deciding state for ratification on June 21, 1788.

LISTINGS: FRENCH AND INDIAN, THE REVOLUTION, THE WAR OF 1812

Acworth

A plaque dedicated to the American Revolution and the War of 1812 in Memorial Park.

Alstead

Minute Man statue in front of the municipal building on Mechanic Street. It was donated by John B. Threllfall in 1999 and was sculpted by Richard Linton of California. It was erected in honor of Nathaniel Sartell Prentice and Simon Brooks.

Antrim

A historical marker dedicated to Samuel Downing, believed to be last surviving Revolutionary soldier in New Hampshire.

Downing was born in Newburyport, Massachusetts, in 1764 and came to Antrim as a boy. He ran away in 1780 at the age of 16 and joined the Second New Hampshire Regiment. He served until the end of the war and returned to Antrim but established permanent residence in Edinburg, New York, where he died in 1867 at the age of 105. Downing lived long enough to have his photograph taken, an unimagined technology during the Revolution. While he was the last New Hampshire Patriot to die, he did not die in the Granite State, and some credit Joel McGregor of Newport with being the oldest New Hampshire Patriot. Downing's marker is located on U.S. Route 202 on the lawn of the Maplehurst Inn, across from the town hall.

Brookline

Bronze plaques dedicated to the American Revolution, the War of 1812 and the Civil War on the town hall lawn.

Candia

In front of the Fitts Museum on High Street, this Civil War monument also lists the names of those who served in the Revolution, the War of 1812, World Wars I and II and the Korean and Vietnam Wars. It was rededicated in 1918 and restored and rededicated in 2007.

Canterbury

The Henry Parkinson plaque on Rum Brook Road.

Center Barnstead

Part of a Civil War monument in the town center. It also includes the Mexican-American War and the War of 1812.

Charlestown

A memorial to Captain Phineas Stevens (French and Indian War) that was dedicated in 1908 on Main Street.

Phineas Stevens knew early on what it meant to be a hero. On August 14, 1723, he, his father and three brothers were ambushed by five hostile Natives. His father, Joseph, managed to escape, but his brothers Samuel and Joseph II were killed. Phineas carried his younger brother Isaac on his back to the camp in Canada, saving him from hunger and exhaustion. His father came to redeem them on August 19, 1725. Stevens later became an Army captain and noted Native fighter, distinguishing himself in the Cape Breton War. He was noted for his defense of Fort No. 4, later named Charlestown, on April 4, 1747, with thirty men against four hundred French and Native troops. In a chilling flashback to his early life, Stevens saw his son, Enos, captured by the enemy forces, though he was later returned. Stevens fought his last campaign with Colonel Robert Nonekton's expedition against the French settlements in Nova Scotia and died during the march to Beau Sejour.

The Liberty Tree Memorial (American Revolution) marker is on Main Street (north of Olcott Lane), located on the left when traveling north.

The liberty elm trees are named after the Liberty Tree, a symbol of the fight for freedom. On August 14, 1765, two effigies were hung from a Boston elm tree in protest of the British government's despised Stamp Act. That elm tree became known as the Liberty Tree and was a meeting place and rallying point for the Sons of Liberty. British soldiers cut it down in August 1775, a last act of violence before their evacuation of Boston. The Charlestown Heritage Commission sponsored the planting of its Liberty Tree as part of a national program, and the plaque was sponsored by the Elm Research Institute of Keene.

There is also a plaque recognizing General John Stark's expedition to Bennington in August 1777. To stop a British invasion from Canada into eastern New York, the New Hampshire legislature commissioned General John Stark to lead a force of 1,500 militiamen. They were assembled and provisioned at Fort No. 4 in Charlestown. They marched west on August 3, and on August 16, they defeated the British at the Battle of Bennington.[5] Erected by the New Hampshire Division of Historical Resources, the marker is located at the intersection of Main Street (New Hampshire Route 12) and Elm Street.

Chester

A memorial is located at Haverhill and Raymond Roads.

Chesterfield

A plaque located in the town hall memorializes the Revolution.

Concord

A John Stark statue is located on the statehouse lawn.[6]

A Battle of Bennington cannon is located at the statehouse.

Cornish

A memorial to Admiral David Glasgow Farragut (War of 1812) was dedicated in 1881 at the Saint-Gaudens National Historic Site.

Admiral Farragut served in the U.S. Navy as a rear admiral, vice admiral and eventually admiral. He is remembered as the hero of the Battle of New Orleans and for his famous phrase at the Battle of Mobile Bay: "Full speed ahead, and damn the torpedoes!"

More torpedoes were damned before Farragut died on August 14, 1870, while visiting Portsmouth, New Hampshire. His other connection to the Granite State is through a piece of sculpture at the Saint-Gaudens Historic Site in Cornish. A statue to Farragut was the first major public commission of Augustus Saint-Gaudens and was unveiled in Madison Square Park on Memorial Day in 1881. The statue, *The Farragut Monument*, was Saint Gaudens's first collaboration with architect Stanford White, which led to a long professional partnership. But by 1934, the original sandstone base had deteriorated, and the City of New York removed the base and had it resculpted in granite. The original base is now on exhibit at the Saint-Gaudens National Historic Site, his summer home and workshop in Cornish. It is topped with a replica of the Madison Square Park statue.

Deerfield

A Revolutionary honor roll plaque is located at Deerfield Public Library on Church Street.

A marker dedicated to Major John Simpson is located at the junction of Routes 107 and 43.[7]

Dover

Alexander Scammell Bridge is located over the Bellamy River. Scammell was a Revolutionary Patriot and soldier who served with distinction through the six years of war, from Bunker Hill to Yorktown. He was wounded and captured at Yorktown and died six days later on October 6, 1781. The bridge was named for Scammell by the general court in 1933, and a plaque was erected in 1991 by the Division of Historical Resources on Boston Harbor Road.

Above: This statue of Admiral David Farragut, a hero of the War of 1812, is on display at the Saint-Gaudens National Historic Site in Cornish. *Sheila Bailey.*

Left: Major John Simpson was an American Revolutionary War soldier from Deerfield and one of several men traditionally described as having fired the first shot on the American side at the Battle of Bunker Hill. *Sheila Bailey.*

Durham

An obelisk-like monument dedicated to John Sullivan, an American general in the Revolutionary War, a delegate to the Continental Congress and governor of New Hampshire, is located on Newmarket Road. It was erected by the State of New Hampshire on the site of the meetinghouse under which the gunpowder taken from Fort William and Mary was stored.

A War of 1812 marker is located on Main Street.

There is a Revolutionary War monument at 44 Main Street. It includes recognition of the capture of Fort William and Mary.

Epsom

A monument dedicated to Major Andrew McClary is located in the town complex on Route 4.[8]

Exeter

A monument dedicated to Brigadier General Enoch Poor (of the American Revolution) was dedicated in 1979; it is located on Newfields Road.

Enoch Poor wasn't born in Exeter, nor did he die there, but he gave his adopted hometown plenty to be proud of. He was born in Andover, Massachusetts. In 1736, he moved to Exeter with his wife, Martha, and worked as a shipbuilder. He joined the Revolutionary forces in 1775. He rose through the ranks, serving as colonel in the Second New Hampshire Regiment and was promoted to brigadier general in February 1777, and in the summer of 1780, he commanded a battalion of light infantry under the Marquis de Lafayette. He distinguished himself in the Battles of Monmouth, Freeman's Farm and Bemis Heights and spent the winter at Valley Forge with General George Washington. Poor was with Washington's forces in August 1780, when Washington crossed into Bergen County, New Jersey, to find food for his men and horses and to wait for the French to join them for a final attack on British-held New York City. Poor never lived to see the battle but instead died from typhus at the age of forty-four in September 1780.

The *Revolutionary Capital*, a plaque noting Exeter's part in the Revolution, was dedicated in 1965 on Front Street.

Enoch Poor wasn't born in Exeter, but he gave his adopted hometown plenty to be proud of. He was born in Andover, Massachusetts, in 1736. He moved to Exeter with his wife Martha, worked as a shipbuilder and joined the Revolutionary forces in 1775. He rose through the ranks, serving as a colonel in the Second New Hampshire Regiment, getting promoted to brigadier general in February 1777 and, in the summer of 1780, commanding a battalion of light industry under the Marquis de Lafayette. *Sheila Bailey*.

Exeter was a Patriot stronghold and served as the provincial capital for New Hampshire during the American Revolution. The American Independence Museum and its Folsom Tavern pay homage to those times with mementoes and events in Downtown Exeter on Water Street.

Fitzwilliam

A plaque honors Brigadier General James Reed, a founder of Fitzwilliam and an active leader in the French and Indian War. He also served as a colonel of the Second Regiment New Hampshire Volunteers at the Battle of Bunker Hill and was a brigadier general in the Continental army. The plaque was erected in 1924 by his descendants at the intersection of New Hampshire Route 119 and Templeton Turnpike.

Fremont

Fremont's Revolutionary soldiers are honored in a monument on the town hall lawn along with those who served in the War of 1812, the Civil War and World War I. The monument was donated by Stephen and Kate Frost in 1920.

Goshen

A plaque in rock honors those who served in the Revolution, the War of 1812, the development of the West, the Civil War, the Spanish-American War and World War I. It was erected by the town in 1923 in front of the Olive Pettis Library.

Hampton Falls

A memorial dedicated to the American Revolution, the War of 1812, the Mexican-American War, the Civil War and the Spanish-American War is located on Lafayette Road.

Hancock

A granite obelisk honors those who served in the French and Indian War, the Revolutionary War, the War of 1812, the Civil War and the First World War in the town square.

Haverhill, North Haverhill and Pike

A Civil War statue on a pedestal also honors the Revolution, the War of 1812 and the Mexican-American and Spanish-American Wars. It was dedicated in 1912 at the intersection of Dartmouth College Highway and Benton Road.

A plaque honors Ebenezer MacKintosh. He was born in Boston and was a veteran of the 1758 Battle of Ticonderoga. He was a known participant in the Boston Tea Party, and for his own and his children's safety, he walked to North Haverhill in early 1774. He later served in the Northern Army under General Gates in 1777. He was a shoemaker by trade and practiced his vocation in North Haverhill for the rest of his life. He was buried nearby in Horse Meadow Cemetery. The marker is located at the intersection of Dartmouth College Highway and Horse Meadow Road and was erected by the Division of Historical Resources.

A memorial to Colonel Charles Johnson stands in Haverhill Corner.

A Rogers' Rangers historic marker is located on Route 10.

Henniker

The Revolution is featured on an obelisk bearing a bust of Colonel Leander Cogswell, a Civil War hero from Henniker. The obelisk memorializes the Revolution, the War of 1812, the Civil War and the First World War. It was dedicated in 1920 and is located between Henniker Library and Cogswell Grammar/Middle School.

Hillsboro

A plaque honoring the Revolution may be seen at 29 School Street.

Holderness

A memorial to the American Revolution is part of a granite monument honoring all wars located outside of a library. The monument was dedicated in 2009.

Hopkinton/Contoocook

The Civil War statue at Rotary Park also includes plaques for those who served in the Revolution and the War of 1812.

Jaffrey

The tribute is part of the Civil War soldier statue in front of library. It also honors the Revolution, the War of 1812, the Mexican-American War and World War I.

Jefferson

The Honor Roll Memorial (dedicated to all wars) was dedicated in November 1999. It is located in the town center across from the Catholic church.

The War Monument was dedicated in 1920. It honors the American Revolution, the Civil War, the Spanish-American War and World War I. It is located at the intersection of Route 2 and Presidential Highway.

Keene

Keene Remembers is located at the intersection of Main and Roxbury Streets. It honors those who served in the Colonial Wars, 1675–1763; the Revolutionary War, 1775–83; the War with England, 1812–14; the War with Mexico, 1846–48; the Mexican Expedition, 1816–18; and World War I, 1917–18.

A plaque at 393 Main Street was donated by the Daughters of the American Revolution (DAR) on April 12, 1902, to mark the "Old Road" to Boston, by which Keene soldiers marched under Captain Isaac Wyman on April 21, 1775.

Littleton

A plaque honoring those who served in the Revolution was donated by the Ellen L. Sanger chapter of the DAR in 1914 and is located on the town green.

Londonderry

A monument to the American Revolution may be seen on the town common. It's a relief of minutemen and includes the outline of the state.

Madison

A monument honoring the Revolution, the War of 1812, the Civil War and the Spanish-American War is located on Village Road.

Manchester

A monument dedicated to John Stark is located in Stark Park on the city's north end.[9]

A monument dedicated to Casimir Pulaski may be seen in Pulaski Park.[10]

Marlow

Plaques honoring the Revolution, the War of 1812, the Civil War, World War I and World War II may be seen at Jones Hall on the village green.

Mason

A plaque was erected in Town Park by the Mason Historical Society honoring Captain Benjamin Mann, who served at Bunker Hill.

Merrimack

A monument is dedicated to Matthew Thornton, a signer of the Declaration of Independence.[11]

Reuben Cummings, a fifteen-year-old drummer boy, died in Battle of Bunker Hill. He was Merrimack's only known casualty. A marker was dedicated to honor him on June 17, 2000, on the grounds of the town's original meetinghouse next to the cemetery at the corner of Meetinghouse and Turkey Hill Roads.

Milford

A monument honors Captain Josiah Crosby and Lieutenant Thompson Maxwell, Revolutionary officers. They were settlers in Monson, which became part of Amherst and then part of Milford. Crosby served with distinction at Bunker Hill and marched to defend Ticonderoga in 1777 and Rhode Island in 1778. Maxwell participated in the Boston Tea Party, the Battles of Lexington and Concord and the Battle of Bunker Hill. While he returned to Massachusetts, he later migrated west and served in the War of 1812. The monument was erected in 1979. It is located on Emmerson Road east of New Hampshire Route 13; it can be seen on the left when traveling east.

Mont Vernon

An honor roll is located on the town green.

Nashua

A memorial to the American Revolution was dedicated in 1910. Nashua, then Dunstable, contributed many men to the Battles of Lexington and Concord and several men to the Battle of Bunker Hill on June 16, 1775, notably drummer boy William Harris; Paul Clogstone, who died from his injuries; and Colonel Ebenezer Bancroft, who was reputed to have killed British major John Pitcairn. The memorial is located in a cemetery in south Nashua.

A memorial to the War of 1812 was dedicated in 2000 and is located in Railroad Square.

New Castle

A memorial at the site of Fort William and Mary commemorates the colonists' resistance to the British effort to seize their munitions in 1774.[12]

Newington

A monument dedicated to the Siege of Louisburg, the American Revolution, the War of 1812 and the Civil War is located on Nimble Hill Road.

Newmarket

A monument to the American Revolution was dedicated in 1922. It is located on the St. Mary Church grounds.

A monument dedicated to Wentworth Cheswell, a Black Patriot who rode with Paul Revere, can be seen on Main Street.

Newport

A monument to Joel McGregor, who served in the American Revolution, was dedicated in 2000 at the intersection of Route 10 and Corbin Road.

McGregor was born in Enfield, Connecticut, in 1760. He enlisted in 1777 and served for five years, including an eight-month stint in the notorious Old Sugar House Prison in New York City. After the war, he settled in Newport and was a seventy-seven-year-resident. He died on October 31, 1861, at the age of 101.

Ossipee

A marker honors Captain John Lovewell's war against the Abenaki at the intersection of New Hampshire Routes 16 and 25.

Peterborough

A memorial to Revolutionary War drummer William Diamond is located on Old Street Road near Second Cemetery.

Plainfield

A memorial honors Black patriot Derrick Oxford.[13]

Portsmouth

A memorial to the Liberty Tree can be seen on Marcy Street.

A plaque remembers the Continental frigate *Raleigh*, which was launched on May 21, 1776, six weeks before the signing of the Declaration of Independence. It was the first American man-of-war built on the Piscataqua River. The plaque was erected in 1926 by the Piscataqua Pioneers. It is located on the side of the John Paul Jones House at 43 Middle Street.

Randolph

On the town green are trifold plaques set in stone. On the left, the Revolution, the War of 1812, the Civil War, World War I and World War II are represented. And to right, the Korean, Vietnam and Persian Gulf Wars and peacetime are represented.

Rye

A memorial to the American Revolution, the War of 1812, the Civil War and the Spanish-American War is located on the town green.

Tamworth

A monument is located in the town center on Route 113.

Temple

A granite Monument to the Heroes of 1775 is located in Rum Brook Park.

Wilmot

Monument Park is located on Village Road.

Woodstock

An engraved stone located in the town common was dedicated on Memorial Day 1910. It is dedicated to the Revolution, the War of 1812 and the Civil War.

A House Restored

The Civil War

*T*he United States wasn't even one hundred years old when it was no longer united. It was a question of slavery to much of the North, a question of states' rights to the defiant South. After four bloody years, the question was answered, more or less, with an emasculated South and a triumphant but sorrowful North. No one really won the Civil War, as a battle-weary and reunited nation was left to pick up the pieces.

George Morrison of Bow, New Hampshire, has spent twenty years studying the monuments and memorials put up for the veterans and casualties of that war. He started in 2010, when he realized the state did not have a comprehensive list of the monuments. His curiosity led to a three-year project and eighteen thousand miles on his car.[14]

Morrison notes that very few memorials to the American Revolution were erected before the Civil War. (This author's guess is that people were too busy establishing a nation.) By the time the Civil War broke out in 1861, according to Morrison, monuments began going up, even before the war's end. The first monuments were usually obelisks with lists of names and sometimes ages and details of service. In 1867, the New Hampshire legislature passed an ordinance allowing towns to raise funds to build memorials and fencing. The fencing was needed to keep livestock away. The state was careful with its funds as always, and most of the memorials were built with town dollars, according to Morrison. In New Hampshire, Washington and Sullivan tie for having the first "town" monuments.

Figural memorials, or "soldier statuary," in Morrison's words, began to appear after the Civil War. Bronze was expensive, but by the 1880s, the cost had gone down, and firms such as the Monumental Bronze Company of Bridgeport, Connecticut, began mass-producing statues. Monumental Bronze's *American Soldier* was placed in eighty locations across thirty states. Stone statuary later came in vogue, with notable examples created in Westerly, Rhode Island, and Barre, Vermont. The style proliferated, and New Hampshire now has sixty-four figural Civil War monuments.

Morrison notes that many cemeteries also feature a memorial to the unknown casualties. Some include the names of people who perished but were buried elsewhere or lost. "The number of these, nearly 130,000, is heartbreaking," Morrison said.

New Hampshire had helped create the Union, and it answered the call to help preserve it.

Its soldiers included men like John J. Railey, who emigrated from Ireland, only to fight for a new country where he wasn't really accepted either. Railey and his family settled in Boston, where they battled the "no Irish need apply" principles on a daily basis. Police arrested a nine-year-old Railey for the heinous crime of playing marbles on the Boston Common on a Sunday. He was sent to reform school on Deer Island before being apprenticed to Robert Eastman of East Concord, New Hampshire. Railey didn't care for life at Eastman's and ran away to find shelter on Zion Hill in Canterbury. But spinsters Polly and Jane Haines saw something in the boy and raised him as their own.

Like the enslaved Derrick Oxford in the Revolution, Railey fought for a country where he wasn't free. But he had a talent the Union needed: he was very good with a gun. He enlisted in Concord on August 25, 1862, and was assigned to the Berdan Sharpshooters, an elite group of marksmen. He saw action in several major battles, including at Gettysburg. Discharged on a medical basis in December 1864, Railey came back to Canterbury and inherited the Haineses' farm.

Most memorials were erected by the town or even the state. But at least one bore witness to a daughter's love for her father and for memories that stand the test of time, even when a statue doesn't. Nellie Bean Zebley was fourteen years old when she saw her father, Loammi Bean, head out to defend the Union. He had recently purchased the 150-acre Nestledown Farm near the Weirs in Laconia, but he was not to farm it or enjoy the fruits of his labors. He was thirty-seven when he enlisted in the Eighth New Hampshire Volunteer Regiment, and he died on October 27, 1862, at the Battle of Georgia Landing in Louisiana.

John J. Railey, an Irish immigrant, fought with Berdan's Sharpshooters in the War Between the States and later came back to his Canterbury farm. *Sheila Bailey*.

In 1894, Nellie, then Mrs. John Zebley, funded a monument in his honor at the New Hampshire Veterans' Association Compound at Weirs Beach. The statue and fountain were dedicated on August 29, 1894. The memorial stood at the gate of the compound and welcomed veterans and their guests for almost forty years. On July 23, 1931, a storm tore through the Lakes Region, and the statue and fountain were destroyed. Bystanders grabbed portions of the statue as souvenirs, and it was considered lost.

But things have a way of finding their way home. In 1978, Robert and Sylvia Newton of Warren found the memorial's plaque in a burned-out cellar hole. They contacted the Laconia Historical Society, and the society put out an APB for descendants of Loammi and Nellie.

Nellie's descendant Richard Tebbetts and his wife, JoAnn, still live in Laconia and were thrilled at the discovery of the plaque. JoAnn, the genealogist of the pair, had done research on Nellie and Loammi and was pleased to learn that a piece of Nellie's tribute still existed.[15]

Though the statue and fountain are gone, the distinctive house-like structures remain, a dignified contrast to the motorcycles, T-shirt shops and arcades in the area.

The Loammi Bean Fountain stood for years at the entrance to the Veterans' Association Campground at Weirs Beach but was destroyed by lightning in 1931. *Warren D. Huse,* The Weirs, *Images of America (Charleston, SC: Arcadia Publishing, 1996).*

The New Hampshire Veterans Association was founded in October 1875 in Manchester at the first reunion and encampment of New Hampshire's Civil War veterans. Brown's Cornet Band provided the entertainment, according to a contemporary news item. The old soldiers found they liked getting together and had their second reunion the following year at Weirs

Landing, now called Weirs Beach, in Laconia. The Boston, Concord and Montreal Railroad made land available to the association for forty-three years and cleared the property for tents and pavilions. One by one, permanent buildings went up, and a veterans' retreat took shape. There would eventually be more than one dozen buildings there, all built in the High Victorian/Queen Anne style. The houses were organized and named according to the soldiers' regiments. The association purchased the eight acres from the railroad in 1924.[16]

Over the years, some of the old frame buildings gave way to fires, hurricanes and public safety issues. The remaining buildings are part of a restoration effort that was started in the 1990s and are in the National Register of Historic Places. The compound is also recognized as the New Hampshire Veterans' Association Historic District.

In the manic atmosphere of Weirs Beach, the Las Vegas of the Lakes Region, the old homes bring a sense of grounding and reflection.

Some of New Hampshire's larger towns funded elaborate stone sculptures with deep emotion and allegorical figures that would foreshadow the monuments of the First World War. Portsmouth's main Civil War monument is located in Goodwin Park off Islington Street.

The Veterans' Association Campground at Weirs Beach, a compound of Queen Anne–style lodges, grew out of the need for Civil War veterans to get together. *Laconia Public Library.*

The Veterans' Association property still welcomes members of its organization to rent a room at Weirs Beach. *Sheila Bailey.*

The larger towns and cities honored their boys in blue with elaborate monuments, such as this one in Goodwin Park in Portsmouth. *Sheila Bailey.*

Portsmouth dedicated its Civil War memorial on July 4, 1888. It features Lady Liberty at the top, with depictions of a Union soldier and sailor on either side. The north side commemorates the Battle of Gettysburg, with the inscription, "In honor of the men of Portsmouth who gave their services on the land and on the sea in the war which preserved the Union of the States this monument is erected by grateful citizens." The south side commemorates the Battle of Antietam and lists other battles in which New Hampshire regiments served, including the Battles of Williamsburg, Fair Oaks, Savage Station, White Oak Swamp, Malvern Hill, Chantilly, South Mountain, Chancellorsville and Wilderness and Sherman's March to the Sea. The west side features the Battle of Fredericksburg and has the Union soldier, and the east side has the sailor along with the *Kearsarge*. The USS *Kearsarge* was a Portsmouth-built warship that sank the CSS *Alabama* in June 1864 off the coast of France. The Lady Liberty figure is cast in the white bronze zinc material that was developed by the Monumental Bronze Company of Bridgeport, Connecticut. The statue is a capsule of Civil War history.

Nashua also paid tribute to its soldiers' ultimate sacrifice with its Soldiers and Sailors Monument.

Nashua's Soldiers and Sailors Monument is located at the junction of Concord, Amherst and Nashville Streets. The cornerstone was laid on May 30, 1889, and the monument was dedicated on October 15 of that year. The monument is a square, castellated column of New Hampshire granite that was quarried near Nashua on a base of Quincy granite. The base is topped with a figure of Victory in classical Roman garb, holding a shield and laurel wreath. The base is also ornamented with bronze figures of a soldier and sailor of the era. Other relief images include the Goddess of Liberty reconciling the South and the North; a depiction of emancipation with a Union soldier extending a scroll to a kneeling figure, presumably an enslaved person; and the sinking of the *Alabama* by the *Kearsarge* on June 19, 1864. A sculpture at the front depicts a saddle draped with cavalry gear, and a sculpture at the rear depicts weapons of the era. Such an elaborate monument had to be a team effort: the design was done by T.M. Perry of Messers Frederick and Field. Perry also carved Victory, erected the monument and did the granite work. S.J. O'Kelley modeled the sailor, which was cast by Melzar Hunt Mosman. Caspar Buberl modeled the soldier, which was cast by the Henry Bonnard Bronze Company. Melzar Hunt Mosman modeled and cast the artillery sculpture, the emancipation relief and two lettered panels. Beattie and Brooks modeled Victory, the cavalry and the sinking of the *Alabama*.

Left: Nashua's *Soldiers and Sailors Monument* has a little bit of everything. *Sheila Bailey*.

Below: Concord's main tribute to its Civil War veterans and casualties is this stately arch guarding the entrance to the statehouse. *Sheila Bailey*.

And Concord's Memorial Arch guards the entrance to the statehouse grounds.

Concord's Memorial Arch was dedicated in July 1892. The text above the arch reads, "In Memory of Her Soldiers and Sailors, the City of Concord builds this memorial." Peabody and Stearns were the architects. The arch stands thirty-three feet, six inches tall, and spans eleven feet and four inches. Its side walls terminate in posts to give it a total width of fifty-three feet. It is made of granite and decorated with classical images, wreaths, shields, bronze lanterns and, at the top, a Civil War Gatling gun.

Manchester pays tribute to its fallen Civil War soldiers with this monument in Veterans' Park.

Manchester's Civil War monument in Veterans' Park was erected by the city in 1878. Its inscription reads, "In honor of the men of Manchester who gave their services in the war which saved the Union and secured equal rights for all under the Constitution." In case some classical scholars come on the premises, a second inscription proclaims, "Et Decorium est

Manchester's main tribute to Civil War veterans and casualties is located in Veterans Park. *Sheila Bailey*.

pro Patria mori Dulce" ("It is sweet and glorious to die for one's country"). Similar to Nashua's and Portsmouth's monuments, the monument in Veterans' Park is rich with allegorical images and statues of those who served and is a history lesson itself. The Manchester monument was under reconstruction at the time of this book's publication, but enough of its spirit shines through the scaffolding.

Notable sculptor Augustus Saint-Gaudens summered in Cornish, and his home is now the Saint-Gaudens National Historic Site. The site features many of his works, including a version of the Colonel Robert Shaw tribute. Shaw was a Massachusetts man from an abolitionist family who commanded the Fifty-Fourth Massachusetts, a unit of Black soldiers, in the War Between the States. Shaw fought both physical and metaphorical battles to get his men the same pay as white enlisted men and to allow them to fight rather than dig ditches. He succeeded, and his men distinguished themselves in combat. But Shaw paid the ultimate price, dying on the battlefield on July 18, 1863. He was buried with his fallen men, and when the Army wanted to move him to a "white man's grave," his staunch abolitionist parents said no. If all this sounds familiar, it's because Matthew Broderick plays Shaw in the movie *Glory*.

Saint-Gaudens wanted to honor Shaw and created a monument at the head of the Boston Common, featuring the Fifty-Fourth and their colonel. But Saint-Gaudens wasn't pleased with his original piece and created a second Shaw memorial, which is on permanent display in one of the outdoor rooms at the historic site.

Perhaps the most prolific image from the War Between the States is the brooding "Single Soldier" atop a shaft of granite, keeping watch over the townspeople from the common or square. Author Castle Freeman wrote in *Yankee* in May 2015, "If you live in New England, then at least one of these soldiers is your neighbor."[17] The "Single Soldier" is usually a freestanding figure of an infantryman cast in stone or bronze, with a forage cap, coat or cape, rifle and bayonet.

The memorials pay tribute to the men who served and to another fact of nineteenth-century life: the Industrial Revolution. Towns with little money could still pay tribute to their war dead with a mass-produced, customizable figure from Ames Manufacturing Company of Chicopee, Massachusetts, or Monumental Bronze of Hartford, Connecticut. Freeman wrote, "'Single Soldiers' were carved in granite, marble or brown stone and cast in bronze or zinc. Many of them were put up in the 1880s or 90s. Some were commissioned as original works, but most were mass-produced, off-the-rack items ordered

Robert Shaw, who commanded the first all-Black regiment, is commemorated in this sculpture by Augustus Saint-Gaudens. *Sheila Bailey*.

from various stonecutters, metal foundries and cemetery monument dealers." "Single Soldiers" could even be ordered from catalogs. Monumental Bronze, whose base price was $450, would often send along an installer. A town could customize the statue according to its local regiment or a particular soldier it wanted to honor, and the company could even distinguish a town's soldier as Union or Confederate with the flip of a few details.

Technological advances in granite and bronze manufacturing allowed for "Single Soldiers" to be made relatively quickly and cheaply. Cara Giamo wrote for Atlas Obscura in August 2017 that Monumental Bronze developed a new white bronze material that it claimed would outlast granite. White bronze wasn't really bronze but was sand-blasted zinc, and when exposed to air, a thin patina supposedly formed over it. It was free from cracking, crumbling or growing moss, according to the advertisements of the time, and towns flocked to buy their silent sentinels. At one point, Monumental Bronze had thirty-one statues spread out among the country's then forty-eight states. The statues didn't crumble, but the company did. It was taken over by the government in 1914 to cast gun mounts and munitions.[18]

Why the "Single Soldier"? A broadcast from WTTW Chicago Public Radio speculates that past war memorials were triumphant and focused on the victory. But the Civil War required something that would "honor the dead, pay tribute to the everyman citizen soldier and tend to the deep wounds of the living."[19]

There are an estimated two thousand "Single Soldiers" in the United States, and New Hampshire has at least sixty-four examples of the style.

Raymond's brooding Civil War soldier was erected in 1910 on the town common and was dedicated on June 21 that same year. The monument cost $2,500 and was made by the Mullins Co. of Salem, Ohio. The statue was fabricated in a similar manner as the Statue of Liberty, with a copper or bronze sheet hammered into a mold. Raymond's is one of two Mullins statues in New Hampshire, according to George Morrison. More than three thousand people attended its dedication. The inscription reads, "Erected in 1910—by the Loyal Sons and Daughters of Raymond in Memory of Her Soldiers and Sailors Who Served in the War that Preserved the Union." The other three sides were inscribed with the names of Raymond men who served during the Civil War. But this soldier suffered the ravages of war even after peace broke out. In the early twenty-first century, an anonymous shooter winged its shoulder. Water entered through the crack and froze, causing damage to the monument. With the help of the Charles W. Canney Camp no. 5, residents raised funds to restore the monument, and it was rededicated on May 30, 2005.

Candia's "Single Soldier" is located across from the Smyth Library on Route 27/High Street. It was a gift from the Honorable Frederick Smyth, a former New Hampshire governor and Candia native. It was dedicated on Friday, October 13, 1893, in a large ceremony, with the members of numerous Grand Army of the Republic (GAR) posts, veterans' associations and state militia units. It was erected on the site where the town's meetinghouse once stood. It was restored in 2007. While the bronze figure is that of a Union soldier, the monument is meant to represent all Candia men and women who gave—or at least offered—their all.

Pembroke's "Single Soldier" watches over the town from a park on busy Route 3.

Wolfeboro's "Single Soldier" stands at the entrance to town.

Other Civil War soldiers made it through the war and lived to give back. Leander Cogswell, member of a prominent Henniker family, distinguished himself in war and peacetime. He enlisted on August 13, 1862, as a private with the Eleventh New Hampshire Volunteers, Company D. He was commissioned as a captain in 1862 and a lieutenant colonel in 1864.

Raymond's *Civil War Soldier* is a focal point on the town common. *Sheila Bailey.*

Candia's Civil War monument was the gift of a former governor. *Sheila Bailey.*

Right: This "Single Soldier" guards the wedge-shaped park on Route 3 in Pembroke. *Sheila Bailey*.

Below: Wolfeboro's "Single Soldier" on the town common represents the fight for freedom, then and now. Born in Rochester, James Foley was raised in Wolfeboro and chose a career as a freelance correspondent, mostly in warzones. He was kidnapped on November 22, 2012, in Syria and murdered on August 19, 2014, in an execution-style killing. His foundation supports journalists and freedom of the press. *Sheila Bailey*.

Leander Cogswell served in the Civil War and then served his town and state. *Sheila Bailey*.

After the war, Cogswell settled back into civilian life. He was the author of *A History of Henniker* and *The History of the Eleventh Regiment*. He served his town and state in the state legislature in 1866, 1867, 1870 and 1871; he served as state treasurer in 1871 and 1872; and he served as a bank commissioner from 1876 to 1881. He served as a justice of the peace, a member of the New Hampshire Historical Society and president of the New Hampshire Antiquarian Society and was a member of the Freemasons. He served locally as a member of the Henniker School Board.

Though the wounds of the Civil War would take another century to heal, men like Cogswell went back to work, and the country strived toward restoring its society to some kind of normal. The Union was whole again. In the nineteenth century, the country also saw action on foreign soil with the Mexican-American War and the Spanish-American War. But nothing prepared the country for the First World War or the loss of an innocence that was never quite regained.

Listings: The War Between the States

Acworth

A Civil War tribute is in Memorial Park.

Alton

A "Single Soldier" is "Dedicated to the memory of those who enlisted from Alton in the War of 1861–65. Died in defense of their country and sleep in unknown graves." It was erected by the M.H. Savage Post of the GAR. Monument Square, Main Street Route 11 on right traveling north.

Alstead

A "Single Soldier" on a granite base can be seen in the town cemetery. It was erected in 1917. There is also a plaque in the village center.

Amherst

The Soldiers' Monument in the town green, which was erected in 1871 and dedicated in 1890, stands on a slice of land that separates Church Street from Middle Street. It was erected to honor the twenty-five soldiers from Amherst who lost their lives in the Civil War. This bronze monument depicts a Union infantryman with his head bowed in contemplation. It was sculpted by Martin Milmore and funded by a legacy from Aaron Lawrence, Esquire.[20] It also honors the Spanish-American War.

Antrim

A "Single Soldier" on a granite base honors the Revolution, the Civil War, the War of 1812 and the Mexican-American War. It was erected by the Ephraim Weston Post 87 of the GAR in 1892. It is located on the common at Antrim Baptist Church.

Ashland

A "Single Soldier" bears the inscription, "In Memory of the Soldiers of Ashland in the War. 1861–1865." It was erected by the town and G.M. Keye's Post of the GAR and the Woman's Relief Corps. It was dedicated on May 30, 1899. The marker is located at the intersection of Main and Depot Streets.

Atkinson

A "Single Soldier" on a granite base is located in the George P. Dow Common on Route 121. It was presented by William C. Todd, a native townsman and former teacher at the Atkinson Academy, in 1890.

Auburn

A block of granite honors the names of Auburn's soldiers on plaques. Soldiers from the Civil War are represented on the south side. It was dedicated in 1976 on Chester Road in Memorial Park.

Barrington

A memorial was erected by Charles W. Canney at Camp no. 5 in May 2006.

Bath

Part of the memorial on the town common honors the Revolution, the War of 1812, the Civil War, World War I and the Korean and Vietnam Wars.

Bennington

A single statue can be found on the town green.

Berlin

A plaque in granite honors Civil War soldiers in Veterans' Park.

Bristol

In the town's square, a memorial plaque is set in the "mouth" of a mortar that was aboard the Union ship *Orvetta*. The plaque lists soldiers from Bristol and also bombardments in which the ship was engaged. It was erected in 1987.

Canaan

A plaque set in a rock on the common is located in the village center.

Candia

A "Single Soldier" stands across from Smyth Library.[21]

Canterbury

There is a Civil War monument on the town green. It pays homage to the regular infantry and also to the four local men who qualified for Berdan's Sharpshooters, including John J. Railey.[22]

Center Barnstead

A "Single Soldier" stands in the town common.

Center Harbor

An honor roll is located at Nichols Library.

Charlestown

A "Single Soldier" also honors the First World War on its west panel. It was dedicated in 1911 on Main Street.

Chester

A "Single Soldier" was erected in 1904 on the town green.

Chesterfield

A monument in the shape of a cross lists World War I casualties listed in the center and Civil War casualties listed on either side. It was erected in 1924 in front of town hall.

Claremont

Soldier at Rest was dedicated on October 19, 1869, on Broad Street.

Colebrook

This "Single Soldier" was dedicated on September 19, 1900, by the Carlos Fletcher Post 57 and is located at the intersection of Routes 3 and 145.

Concord

Concord's Memorial Arch is located in the statehouse plaza.[23]

The Grand Army of the Republic Memorial is located on statehouse grounds. It was erected on April 9, 1942. Its sundial is inscribed with, "We live in deeds, not years."

The George Hamilton Perkins Monument is located at the rear of the statehouse. George Hamilton Perkins was born in Contoocook and graduated from the U.S. Naval Academy with the class of 1856. He spent the first several months of the Civil War on the *Sumter*, taking part in antislavery

This sundial on the statehouse lawn in Concord commemorates fallen Civil War soldiers. *Sheila Bailey*.

patrols. He was assigned to the USS *Cayuga* and performed distinguished service in the Battle of New Orleans and while securing the lower Mississippi River area. He was at the wheel of the *Cayuga* when it was assaulted by eleven Confederate warships and when it was the first boat sent ashore to demand the surrender of New Orleans. While commanding the *Chickasaw*, he performed aggressive and effective actions in the Battle of Mobile Bay in August 1864 and was instrumental in the capture of the Confederate ship *Tennessee*. He died in Boston in October 1899. The sculpture was made by Daniel Chester French.[24]

A plaque noting the location of a Civil War mustering camp is located at the corner of Airport and Loudon Roads.

Cornish

The Robert Shaw/Fifty-Fourth Regiment Memorial (Civil War) was dedicated in 1897 at the Augustus Saint-Gaudens National Historic Site.[25]

Derry

The East Derry Civil War Monument was dedicated in 1888 and is located on East Derry Road.

Dover

A monument (Civil War) was dedicated on October 19, 1912. It's an obelisk with a "Single Soldier" at the top; the soldier is accompanied by a furled flag and a soldier and sailor at the base. The monument is located on Locust Street.

Dublin

This memorial (Civil War) was dedicated in 1870 at the Main Street Schoolhouse.

Enfield

The Civil War Monument is located on Route 4 near High Street in Veterans' Memorial Park.

Exeter

A boulder and plaque honor General Gilman Marston, a Civil War veteran, at the Arbor Street entrance to Exeter Cemetery.

The public library on Front Street was dedicated to the Civil War heroes and now houses the historical society.

Exeter's public library on Front Street was built in 1896 to honor the town's men who died defending freedom in the War Between the States. It is currently occupied by the Exeter Historical Society. *Sheila Bailey*.

Farmington

The Soldiers Monument (Civil War) was dedicated in 1890 and is located in James B. Edgerly Memorial Park.

Franklin

A plaque honors Civil War veterans on Soldiers Memorial building, now city hall.

Soldiers Memorial hall (1892) was itself a memorial to the Civil War and is now city hall.

Franklin's Soldiers Memorial Building, erected to honor the town's participation in the War Between the States, is now used as the city hall and also bears memorials to other wars. *Sheila Bailey.*

Gilmanton

The grave of Edwin Sewall Nelson, New Hampshire's last Civil War veteran to die, on May 15, 1938, is located in Pine Grove Cemetery.

Goffstown

The Soldiers Monument (Civil War) was dedicated in 1916 on Main Street. It was donated by Henry W. Parker.

Hampstead

A Civil War monument includes a "Single Soldier" and an honor roll on Main Street (Route 121).

Haverhill

The Soldiers of Haverhill Memorial (Civil War) was dedicated in 1912 at the intersection of Dartmouth College Highway and Benton Road. It also honors the Revolution, the War of 1812 and the Mexican-American and Spanish-American Wars.

Hill

A tribute is located in Veterans' Park.

Hopkinton

The Soldiers Monument (Civil War) is located in a triangular park in the center of Hopkinton Village.

Keene

The Soldiers Monument (Civil War) is a bronze statue of an infantryman that was created by Martin Milmore, an Irish-born sculptor. Its legend reads, "Keene will cherish in perpetual honor the memory of her sons who fought for liberty and the integrity of the Republic, 1861–1865." The monument is located in Central Square. Milmore also sculpted the Civil War statues for Amherst, Claremont and Peterborough.[26]

Laconia

An obelisk in Veterans Square honors those who served in the War Between the States.

Lancaster

The Soldiers and Sailors Monument (Civil War) was constructed in 1907 on the site of the town's first meetinghouse (1784), now Soldiers Park on Prospect Street.

An obelisk in the town center honors Colonel Edward Cross, who served at the Battles of Rappahannock, Antietam, Fredericksburg and Gettysburg. Cross is also honored at Gettysburg, where he died on July 2, 1863.

Lebanon

A monument to the Civil War is located in Soldiers Memorial Hall; the hall was built by veterans of the Civil War between 1886 and 1890 and was formerly used as the town's library. The memorial chamber inside has names of Lebanon's Civil War veterans. A "Single Soldier" stands outside the building at 31 North Park Street.

Lempster

A memorial is located at the historical society.

Littleton

A Soldiers and Sailors Monument (Civil War) and a "Single Soldier" on pedestal were donated in 1911 by George Henry Tilton. The memorial was originally located at the town hall, but residents feared damage, and it was moved to the West Main Street Cemetery in 1957.

Londonderry

A Soldiers Monument (Civil War) and a "Single Soldier" were erected in 1884 in the town common.

Lyme

A Soldiers Monument (Civil War) and a "Single Soldier" can be seen in the town green.

Manchester

A Soldiers Monument is located in Veterans' Park on the corner of Elm and Merrimack Streets.[27]

Marlborough

A Soldiers Monument (Civil War) is located in front of the Frost Free Library.

Meredith

Major Bedee's Civil War/Twelfth Regiment Statue and a "Single Soldier" can be found on Main Street, on the right when traveling south. The memorial is located at the front entrance to the Meredith Public Library on the greensward.

Merrimack

A Soldiers and Sailors Monument (Civil War) was dedicated in 1892 opposite the town hall on Baboosic Lake Road.

Milford

A Civil War memorial was dedicated on April 27, 1870, in Milford Town Hall.

An Unknown Soldier Memorial (Civil War) was dedicated in 1892 in the West Street Cemetery.

Milton

A Soldiers Monument (Civil War) is located at 8 Steeple Street.

Nashua

A Soldiers and Sailors Monument (Civil War) was dedicated in 1888 at the intersection of Concord, Amherst and Nashville Streets.[28]

A Major General John Foster Monument (Civil War) is located in Foster Square at the corner of Orange and Locke Streets.

Newport

A memorial is located on the town green.

New Durham

A memorial was dedicated in May 2004 in front of town hall.

New Ipswich

A memorial to all wars is located on the town green.

Pembroke

A "Single Soldier" is located at the intersection of Route 3 and Broadway.[29]

Peterborough

A "Single Soldier" is located at the former GAR Hall.

Pittsfield

A Soldiers and Sailors Monument (Civil War) was dedicated in 1890 in Dustin Park.

Plaistow

A monument is located on the town green in Pollard Square Park, next to town hall. The monument was built in 1908 and bears the names of 105 Plaistow veterans. The monument was donated by Arthur G. Pollard and was maintained by the Village Improvement Society, a group of civic-minded women in the late 1800s and early 1900s.

Portsmouth

A monument honors General Fitz John Porter, a career officer in the U.S. Army who served as a Union general during the War Between the States. He was court-martialed after his alleged performance at the Battle of Bull Run and charged with two violations of the Articles of War: disobeying an order from a superior and misbehaving in front of the enemy. He was finally reinstated to the Army but worked for twenty-five years after the war to restore his reputation. The sculpture was made by James Edward Kelly and dedicated in 1906 in Haven Park.

A Soldiers and Sailors Monument (Civil War) was dedicated on July 4, 1888, in Goodwin Park.[30]

Plymouth

A granite monument is located in Town Park.

Raymond

Raymond's brooding Civil War soldier was erected in 1910 on the town common and dedicated on June 21 that same year.[31]

Rochester

A granite monument was erected by the town in 1885. The memorial can be reached from Common Street just south of South Main Street (State Route 108) and is on the right when traveling south. The monument and marker are located at the center of Rochester Common. The common was used as a staging ground for Revolutionary soldiers from Rochester, and the four cannons originally included with the monument were melted down for artillery in World War II.

Rollinsford

A Soldiers Monument was dedicated on May 30, 1903, in Morton Park.

Salem

A monument is located in Pine Grove Cemetery.

Seabrook

A Soldiers Monument and a "Single Soldier" are located in the town's cemetery.

Springfield

A Soldiers Monument is located in the town hall.
A monument is located in Pleasant View Cemetery.

Stoddard

A monument was dedicated on August 24, 1917, during Old Home Day. It was donated by James H. Hunt, a Stoddard native who was a veteran of the Civil War. Eighteen Civil War veterans attended the dedication in front of the church in the town center.

Stratham

A war monument was dedicated on October 12, 1920, honoring sixty-two men who served the country in the Civil War, and thirty-three men and three women who served the world in World War I. The monument is located in Stratham Hill Park.

Sullivan

The small western town of Sullivan has the distinction of putting up the first authorized war monument in New Hampshire, after the legislature passed an act in 1867 authorizing towns to erect monuments. Sullivan's monument, remembering ten young men who gave their lives for the Union, was dedicated on July 4, 1867, in Sullivan Center.[32]

Sutton

A "Single Soldier" was dedicated in 1890 in Town Park.

Tamworth

A trifold monument to the Revolution, the War of 1812, the Civil War and the Spanish-American War was dedicated in 1929 in Veterans' Park.

Tilton/Northfield

A Soldiers Monument was erected in 1889 by the citizens of Tilton. A "Single Soldier" on a stepped granite base is located at the intersection of West Main Street (U.S. 3) and Winter Street. It can be seen on the right when traveling west on West Main Street.

Troy

An obelisk in memory of the "defenders of the Union" was erected in 1915 by the Sons of Veterans and Sons of Veterans Auxiliary. The memorial is located at the intersection of Central Square and Mill Street.

Wakefield

The Gaffney Library was named for Charles Gaffney, who was born in Ossipee in September 1843. He attended Ossipee schools and then academies in Sandwich and Lebanon, Maine, before reading law. He enlisted in the Civil War at the age of eighteen and was given the rank of second lieutenant. Severely wounded at Petersburg, Virginia, he was mustered out of the Army as a captain. He stayed in Washington and worked as clerk for the Senate Committee for Naval Affairs for eight years. He attended Columbia College Law School in the evenings and graduated in 1868. He died at the age of fifty-five, bequeathing $5,000 for a library in Wakefield.

Warner

Warner honors the Civil War with a "Single Soldier" and a memorial to General Walter Harriman. There are also plaques for the Spanish-American War and the War of 1812 in the town green on Main Street.

Warren

A Civil War Soldiers Monument was dedicated in 1913. The dedication was made during Warren's 150th Anniversary. The monument list soldiers from several wars, including the Civil War, the Spanish-American War and the Mexican-American War. It is located near the Mt. Mooselaukee Health Center.

Washington

A memorial obelisk (Civil War) was dedicated on September 13, 1867, in the town square. It is the oldest monument in New Hampshire. It was built before the legislature authorized towns to raise money for monuments, but Sullivan's was dedicated first.[33]

Weirs Beach

The Loammi Bean Fountain was dedicated on August 29, 1894.[34]

This part of Laconia is also home to the New Hampshire Veterans' Association complex.[35]

Westmoreland

A GAR grave marker honors Major General John Sedgwick, who was killed in action in May 1864 in Spotsylvania, Pennsylvania. The marker is located on Glebe Road.

Whitefield

A memorial is located in the town common.

Wilmot

A Civil War monument, the Wilmot Soldiers Monument, is located in the heart of Wilmot Village on Village Road. The land for the monument park was purchased from several owners by Luvia M. Carr, Addie R. White, J.H. Greeley and Benjamin Emons for $210 and was deeded by them to the Town of Wilmot in 1919.

Winchester

A "Single Soldier" with a plaque was erected in 1908. The memorial can be seen at the intersection of Main Street (State Highway 119) and Richmond Road (State Highway 119) and is on the right when traveling north on Main Street.

Wolfeboro

A "Single Soldier" on top of a column with a furled flag stands at the intersection of South Main (New Hampshire Route 109) and Center Streets (New Hampshire Route 28) and can be seen on the right.[36]

Over There and Over Here

The First World War

*I*n the first decade of the new century, few Americans were familiar with Europe. Unless their families had wealth and sent them on the grand tour, most young men and especially women in America felt destined to live out their lives on the family farm, in the factory or in the retail store. America at the dawn of the twentieth century was a sunlit summer afternoon of fishing at the creek, even if you lived nowhere near the creek. Neighbors chatted over fences or from front porches. It was a time of innocence, with small-town life as regulated as a clock and the storied "amber fields of grain," a sense of progress with automobiles, nickelodeon shows and telephones—but not too much and not too fast.

The assassination of an Austrian archduke changed all of that and plunged most of Europe into a bitter war starting in 1914.

The war began when Gavrilo Princip, a Bosnian Serb nationalist and member of the Black Hand Military Society, assassinated the Austro-Hungarian heir Archduke Ferdinand in Sarajevo. Austria-Hungary issued an ultimatum to Serbia. Serbia's reply did not satisfy Austria-Hungary, and both nations poised themselves for war. A network of European countries took up alliances—and arms. By July 1914, Europe was divided: the Triple Entente comprised France, Russia and Britain, and the Triple Alliance included Germany, Hungary and Italy. Other nations staked out their positions, and in the end, Europe was divided. The Allied Powers included the United Kingdom, France, Russia, Italy, Japan, Portugal and the Balkan states. The Central Powers comprised the German empire, the Austro-Hungarian Empire, the Ottoman Empire and Bulgaria.

America held off for three years—it wasn't our fight. But eventually, President Woodrow Wilson, spurred by the German sinking of American ships, declared war in April 1917, and America joined the Allied Powers.

Few American doughboys knew what they were getting into. Spurred by patriotism and by the fear of the coward's "white feather," they joined up in a surge of nationalism and were soon on their jaunty way to "whup the kaiser." They would indeed whup the kaiser, with results that reached far into the twentieth and twenty-first centuries—for better or for worse. And a generation of young men met death in places they couldn't pronounce.

It was the first war fought with modern technology and innovations. These armies used motorized ambulances and telephones, and this war spawned the tank and the dreaded mustard gas. It was a time of progress for women, who left their home states and country to nurse the wounded, and it brought a hunger for change to the Black soldiers, who found a respect in Europe that did not follow them home.

New Hampshire did its share, contributing some of its best and brightest. Some were staunch Yankee stock whose families had been in this country since its founding. Some, like Manchester's Christos Kalivas, were new Americans who picked up a rifle to defend their adopted country. Some were on the front lines, even if they'd never fired a gun before. Others, such as Plainfield's Harry Thrasher, gave their specific talents to the cause—and in some cases, they gave their lives. Thrasher, a professional artist and sculptor, was recruited to work on camouflage but took a German shell and died.

A grateful country and state honored their losses and determined that these would be the last.

Berlin, the North Country's largest city, erected a Soldiers and Sailors Monument in 1921. Raymond Averill Porter received the commission, and the amount allotted toward its construction was $6,720. Porter designed a concrete base, with a shaft of pink granite and a bronze relief of a life-sized woman representing Liberty. She wore a robe and sandals and carried a wreath. Six thousand people attended the unveiling on a rainy July 19, and the statue was unveiled by the town's remaining Civil War veterans.

Exeter cherishes its history and its memories as much as any town in New Hampshire, and no less than a world-famous sculptor—and native son—would do for the town's memorial to the Great War. Daniel Chester French, most noted for the Lincoln Memorial in Washington, D.C., created the monument in full allegorical style. The land at the corner of Lincoln and Front Streets was donated by Alice Gale Hobson in memory of her father, General Stephen M. Gale, and was dedicated on July 4, 1922.

No less than Daniel Chester French sculpted Exeter's World War I monument in Gale Park. *Sheila Bailey.*

French's tribute has a little bit of everything: a doughboy, a statuesque figure interpreted as his loving mother guiding him and a fluttering flag. The inscription reads, "With veneration of those who died. Gratitude of those who lived. Trust in the patriotism of those who came after. The town of Exeter dedicates this memorial. To her sons and daughters of the World War." While there are no angels or shrouded figures of death included in this sculpture, the mother figure carries out the emotionalism of the period.

Few war memorials in New Hampshire for any war can match the pedigree of *Buddies*, a monument in downtown Jaffrey. This relief of a doughboy carrying a wounded buddy was sculpted by Danish artist Viggo Brandt-Erichsen, and it has a different kind of love story at its core.

Brandt-Erichsen met Dorothy Caldwell, a wealthy American, while working in Paris in the 1920s. Caldwell had summered in Jaffrey as a child. She died giving birth to their daughter and so did the child but not before she asked Brandt-Erichsen to have them buried in Jaffrey. So, the young Dane sailed for America with Dorothy's and the baby's ashes in tow. He stayed in Jaffrey and spent two years creating a memorial for Dorothy and the child that can be seen in the town's Old Burial Ground. The town quickly adopted Brandt-Erichsen. In his beret and artist's smock, he became a familiar sight around Jaffrey.

Brandt-Erichsen wanted to give back to the town that his Dorothy had never forgotten. In 1928, he offered to create—pro bono—a memorial to the First World War heroes. He used a forty-ton boulder for the stone, which was transported on rollers over frozen ground to the town common. The trip took six weeks. The boulder was placed behind an existing World War I honor roll that was erected in 1919, and volunteers built a rough shack to protect the sculptor from the New England weather. He worked for two years, using electric chisels and hand tools. He used two local veterans as models, and the inscription at the bottom says simply, "Buddies."

The monument was dedicated on Armistice Day, November 11, 1930, before an estimated crowd of seven thousand people. Speakers included the governor and General Clarence Edwards, the commander of the Twenty-Sixth (Yankee) Division, under whom most of Jaffrey's men had served. The monument was unveiled by Carrie Humiston, the mother of the only Jaffrey soldier who was killed in action.

Manchester, New Hampshire's largest city, has a memorial to match in the appropriately named Victory Park. The centerpiece is a large granite column topped by a bronze *Victory* statue, a winged female form with her arms lifted to display a flagpole and laurel wreath. But wait, there's more: she's perched on a globe surrounded by four eagles. Two large bronze sculptures flank the base. On one side are a soldier, a sailor and a larger figure of Columbia with a helmet, breastplate, shield and sword. The other side holds a female figure, her face almost completely obscured under a hooded cloak. The woman's hand supports her head as she rests against a large, inscribed tablet with the following: "In memory of the Manchester men who died in the Great War that the World be made safe for Democracy....In a Righteous Cause, they have won Immortal Glory and Have Nobly served their Nation in Serving Mankind." Lucien H. Gosselin was the sculptor, and the monument was dedicated in 1929. The monument carries the themes of many World War I tributes—the allegorical figures, the somber air and the deep emotion. No one can miss the point of the Victory Park monument. And from its location at the intersection of Chestnut, Amherst, Pine and Concord Streets, no one ever will.

Above: Jaffrey's *Buddies Monument* has its own love story at its core. *Sheila Bailey*.

Right: Manchester's own Lucien Gosselin created the World War I memorial, a feast of allegory and emotion, in Victory Park. *Sheila Bailey*.

Christos N. Kalivas Memorial Park was dedicated on March 23, 2002, in honor of Manchester's first Greek American to die in the Great War. A member of the U.S. Army, Kalivas died on October 8, 1918. He was a private in the First Division, Sixteenth Infantry and was buried in the Meuse-Argonne American Cemetery in Romagne, France.

Kalivas was born in September 1888 in Dolo, Greece, and immigrated to America in 1908, settling in Manchester and seeking a better life for the wife and daughter he left behind. He worked as a "heel sorter" at the Mcelwain Shoe Factory. Though he worked ten years, he was never able to send for his family. He was inducted into the Army on May 24, 1918, and served in the Meuse-Argonne Campaign.

The park was renamed Kalivas Park on May 26, 1940. A fundraising drive was started to raise the money needed for a monument, but it was halted in April 1942 after $5,000 was raised. Fundraising resumed after the Second World War. A monument, a bronze plaque bearing his likeness, was finally erected in 1959. The monument is thirty feet tall with bronze sculptures representing the Army, Navy and Marines against a Doric column. Adio diBicarri sculpted the piece. More than four thousand people attended its dedication.

Kalivas is also memorialized in a book, *The Spirit of Kalivas Park*, which was written by fellow Greek Americans Spiros Plentzas and Dr. Chris D. Kehas and published in 2005.

Kalivas Park, formerly known as Park Common, was a hub of Greek American activity in the city, similar to a *plateia* or village square, because of the Greek-owned businesses surrounding it. The renaming and rededication of the park serves not only as a memorial to Kalivas and his heroism but also as a tribute to Manchester's Hellenic community.[37]

Manchester's Harriman Park was originally named East Side Park. Emma S. Richard donated the land on October 31, 1905. The park was rededicated on November 15, 1922, in honor of Lieutenant Lynn H. Harriman. Harriman was the son of Boyd and Nellie Harriman and was originally from Warner. Lieutenant Harriman served in the 101st Infantry in World War I and died in May 1918, four days after being mortally wounded in combat near the Humbert Plantation in France. A citation from the War Department noted that "despite being mortally wounded, he fought on" and led his men with "determination and courage." Lieutenant Harriman posthumously received the French Croix de Guerre and the American Distinguished Service Cross for his bravery. He was buried in Warner. Harriman Park is located on the corner of Lake Avenue and Hall Street and

Christos Kalivas, the first Greek American from Manchester to die in World War I, has this monument and a park named after him. *Sheila Bailey.*

the corner of Hall and Central Streets. The park comprises 0.41 acres and includes a playground and a basketball court.[38]

Manchester's Franco-Americans who served are honored at Mount Calvary Cemetery, 474 Goffstown Road, with a bronze relief figure of a French legionnaire wearing the uniform of the Jutras American Legion Post 43. The image holds a flagstaff with the flag swirling behind him. The monument also includes two palm branches and a flower. The granite base is shaped like a Gothic arch on a three-tiered base flanked by buttresses and topped with a cross. The base includes the seals of United States and New Hampshire placed over bronze olive branches. The sculptor was Lucien H. Gosselin, and it was dedicated on October 8, 1939, in honor of Manchester's Franco-Americans who served in the Great War.[39]

Tiny Marlow also did its bit in the Great War, sending eight young men to serve. These men are memorialized in a granite monument in front of the historic Jones Hall. A resident, Agnes Grant Phelps, left $1,900 to the town for the creation of a memorial. Martin M. Comolli of Milford received the commission. He was a veteran of the Great War, and his *American*

Manchester's Franco-Americans who served are honored at Mount Calvary Cemetery with a bronze relief figure of a French legionnaire wearing the uniform of the Jutras American Legion Post 43. *Sheila Bailey.*

Doughboy is a personal statement. Comolli's attention to detail shows in the soldier's scabbard, field bag, canteen and even the hobnails on his boots. George Mastin, the last living Civil War veteran from Marlow, attended the dedication on June 1, 1930. The total cost of the memorial was $2,237.25, and the town made up the difference from Phelps's bequest. The monument was upgraded and rededicated on Memorial Day in 1989 with new granite curbing, shrubs and benches.[40]

Harry Thrasher was the only person from Plainfield to die in the Great War, and he was buried in France. He was an artist, sculptor and fellow of the American Academy in Rome and entered the war as part of a group of artists recruited to paint camouflage. Thrasher had ties to the Cornish community, Maxfield Parrish and especially Augustus Saint-Gaudens, with whom he studied. He then studied at the American Academy in Rome from 1911 to 1914, when his former mentor Parrish recommended him to the secretary of the Army for the Camouflage Corps. Thrasher died on August 11, 1918. And though he never returned home, his work survives at the Metropolitan Museum of Art in New York City.

Left: Smaller towns, such as Marlow, also remembered their doughboys. *Sheila Bailey*.

Right: Plainfield's Harry Thrasher, an artist on the rise, was recruited for his artistic talents to help with camouflage but gave his life as gallantly as a draftee. He was Plainfield's only casualty, and his name is kept in gold on the town monument at the Read Memorial Library. *Plainfield Historical Society*.

Thrasher was part of a group looking for fresh gun positions, according to community member Virginia Drye, and they wanted to go into a valley where the Germans were shelling and gassing the French and their livestock. The Germans had killed fifty men and two hundred horses, Drye said. Thrasher was hit, and a colleague, Barry Faulkner, wrote, "I believe he died instantly."

Drye first became aware of Thrasher about fourteen years ago, when the town sponsored a scavenger hunt. One of the items was the World War I memorial at the Philip Read Library, and Drye remembers seeing Thrasher's name in gold as the only member of the Plainfield community to die in the war. "He caught my eye, and I wanted to do something to preserve his memory," Drye recalled. "There were a lot of cool people on that list, but Harry stood out." She researched the young artist and planned to lay a wreath in his honor on the town monument for the one hundredth anniversary of the Armistice on November 11, 2018. However, "Things just snowballed," she said.

Former state senator Peter Burling's house straddles the Cornish/Plainfield town line, with the former Thrasher residence next door. "Peter asked me, 'What are you going to do about Harry?'" Drye recalled. And she knew she had to do something for him individually in his hometown. "There's a bench with his name on it in Rome, but there was nothing here," she said. Drye, Burling, the town administrator and selectmen worked on a plan and wording for Harry's memorial at 62 Thrasher Road, his former home, and it was dedicated on August 11, 2018, one hundred years to the day after his death. Drye's friend Julien Icher, a native of France, was touring America at the time, documenting all the places the Marquis de Lafayette had visited in 1825, and Drye had him read the places where Thrasher served.

Though chisels clanged and copper sizzled, New Hampshire's monument wasn't always a statue or even a granite column. Portsmouth's Memorial Bridge, dedicated in 1923, spanned a century of seacoast life. Built as a joint venture between Maine and New Hampshire to honor the dead from the Great War, it was dedicated by five-year-old Eileen Foley, who was later to serve eight terms as the mayor of Portsmouth, attend the closing of the bridge in 2011 and return for the opening of the new bridge in 2013. The bridge served Portsmouth and Kittery, Maine, well into the early twentieth century but began to show signs of wear until vehicles of more than twenty tons were prohibited. But the sacrifices continue to be remembered, with a large plaque salvaged from the original bridge reading, "A Memorial to

Left: Resident Virginia Drye was instrumental in getting a marker for Thrasher installed near his former home on Thrasher Road. It was dedicated in August 2018. *Virginia Drye.*

Right: Julien Icher, Virginia Drye, Peter Burling and Colonel Stuart Hodgeman, U.S. Army retired, at the dedication of the Thrasher marker. *Virginia Drye.*

Portsmouth's Memorial Bridge was erected to honor those who served in the Great War. *Sheila Bailey.*

the Sailors and Soldiers of New Hampshire who gave their lives in the World War 1917–1919." And a nearby monument to veterans of all wars is mounted on the granite blocks that supported the old bridge.

Nashua's Amedee Deschenes left not only his own legacy but also that of a veterans' park for all wars and all branches. Private First Class Deschenes was born on Valentine's Day 1895 in Nashua's French Hill section. Educated in local parochial schools, Deschenes was working at the Jackson Mills when he enlisted. He went overseas with the Twenty-Sixth Yankee Division. Deschenes was already a hero before his death. On June 16, 1918, he was manning an outpost with four other soldiers when a force of six hundred Germans advanced under a barrage of gunfire, not aware of the little outpost. Deschenes opened fire, causing the Germans to retreat, and was honored by the French with the Croix de Guerre. He met his own death on September 26, 1918, while fighting in Saint-Mihiel. He was gassed and died on October 1 in a French hospital and was buried in France.

On November 11, 1920, his hometown honored him with a monument to his service and the naming of a veterans' park at Railroad Square. Since

Above: This memorial, a stone's throw from the new Memorial Bridge, uses granite trusses from the first bridge to honor all of Portsmouth's members of the armed forces. *Sheila Bailey.*

Right: The *Deschenes Oval* in Nashua's Railroad Square is named for Amedee Deschenes, a Nashua man who made the ultimate sacrifice in the First World War. *Sheila Bailey.*

that day, other memorials have grown up around his, paying tribute to World War II and the Korean, Vietnam, Persian Gulf and Iraq Wars.

A statue in Rindge, technically unfinished, speaks eloquently to the loss felt in this and all wars. The model for the *Ecce Homo* statue may be found in the Cathedral of the Pines, a memorial garden in Rindge.[41] Sculptor Leonard Craske, best known for his memorial statue of a Gloucester fisherman, also worked on plans for a World War I monument that featured a statue of Jesus on the cross looking down at a dying soldier.

Leonard Craske, best known for his statue of the *Gloucester Fisherman*, designed *Ecce Homo*, but the full statue was never completed. A model is on display at the Cathedral of the Pines in Rindge. *Sheila Bailey*.

The soldier wore no rank or insignia that would designate his country or branch of service. Craske tentatively titled the piece *Ecce Homo* ("Behold, the Man"). He was commissioned by the federal government to create the statue for Arlington National Cemetery, but for reasons unknown, Craske broke the contract. Craske did have a working model, and he visited Cathedral of the Pines and talked with founders Douglas and Sibyl Sloane about the monument. He changed his will to leave *Ecce Homo* to the cathedral but died three weeks later. His working model of *Ecce Homo* can still be seen in the cathedral's Peter J. Booras Museum.

New Hampshire lost 697 residents in the Great War, young men gone too soon and memorialized by their state with a bronze plaque in the statehouse. Countless others came home with an arm or leg missing or the invisible wounds later to be known as "shell shock." Their towns honored them with everything from stark lists of names to florid allegorical statuary. Some towns planted trees in their honor, a subtle recognition of the burned-out Europe where they fought. Most were not buried at home but under plain white crosses in places their families could never visit.

The ones who came home whole took their places in the factories, farms and general stores. The ones who came home maimed found something to do with their altered resources, and the ones who came home tortured inside hid it. Though they and their grateful country tried to renew those sunlit days from before the war, it never happened, because they knew too much.

Listings: World War I

Acworth

A monument stands in Memorial Park.

Alton

There is an honor roll dedicated to those who served in World War I, World War II and the Korean War, with a special notation for those who made the "supreme sacrifice." It was erected in 1959 by the citizens of Alton. It is located in Monument Square on Main Street (NH Route 11) and can be seen on the right.

Alstead

Alstead's World War I and World War II monuments were donated by the American Legion Britton-Porter Post and VFW Whiton-Pelton posts and dedicated on August 14, 1949. They were destroyed by the October 2005 flood, and the town rebuilt these monuments along with monuments to the Korean, Vietnam and post-Vietnam wars. They were dedicated in 2008 in the town center.

Amherst

A plaque dedicated in 1920 listing those who served with two "starred" deaths. The plaque is nestled in a boulder and located on the town green. Like many of the towns in the aftermath of the war, Amherst listed the conflict as "The War." The boys were home, and the citizenry believed there would never be another overseas war. They were wrong.

Antrim

A plaque lists those who served, along with starred deaths, in "the World War." It is decorated with a relief of soldiers going over the top. The plaque was dedicated on Memorial Day in 1922 and is located in front of the James Tuttle Library and Historical Society.

Atkinson

A memorial plaque lists the names of those involved in "the World War." The 1920 town meeting voted to appropriate enough money for "a memorial for our brave boys who were in the war," according to town historian Adele Dillon. It took "a couple of years" to raise the $550 needed, and the granite column was dedicated on November 11, 1912. Atkinson also named two streets after its two casualties, Leroy and Maurice Avenues. The historical society made the World War II and Korean War monuments to mirror the World War I monument, and they all stand on the lawn of the Atkinson Historical Society.[42]

Auburn

A memorial plaque was dedicated in 1920 at 47 Chester Road. It includes an allegorical figure proclaiming "Victory" and "Peace"—little did they know.

Barnstead

The Earl B. Clark Legion Hall, a former church, is dedicated to the memory of a Barnstead man killed in the Argonne Forest in World War I.

Bath

A plaque on a granite column was dedicated in 1923. The plaques on either side also represent those who died in World War II, the Korean War, the Vietnam War, the Revolutionary War, the Civil War, the War of 1812 and the Mexican-American War. The plaques are located at the intersection of West Bath and Lisbon Roads.

Bedford

A memorial to World War I and the Spanish-American War is located in Old Town Hall on Bedford Center Road.

The Stevens-Buswell building was named for Willis Stevens, who died of an infection on January 13, 1917, in the Naval Hospital at Chelsea, Massachusetts, and Frank Buswell, who died on September 27, 1918, of influenza. Both were in active service when they died.

Belmont

A bronze plaque with relief work depicts an allegorical figure representing America or Columbia, in flowing robes. One hand holds an American flag; the other rests on a shield. The figure is flanked by a kneeling World War I infantryman and sailor, with an eagle soaring above the three figures. A roll of honor recognizes those who served in World War I, the Civil War and the Spanish-American War; and a roll of honor on the rear recognizes those who served in World War II and the Korean and Vietnam Wars. This memorial was produced by Liberty Bronze Works and was donated by Moses Sargent at a cost of $5,000. It was dedicated on Armistice Day in 1919 at the intersection of Church Street and Church Hill Road.

Berlin

The North Country's largest city erected a Soldiers and Sailors Monument in 1921.[43]

Bethlehem

An honor roll includes the name of one nurse, Alice Jobin, on the town green.

Bradford

The Memorial Honor Roll (World War I and World War II) was donated by Gaylord Cummings in 1972. It includes three nurses, Mabel Cressy, Gretchen Cressy and Audrey Sargent, and is located at town hall.

Bristol

An honor roll is located in the town square.

Brookline

Bronze plaques for World War I and the Spanish-American War are located in town hall.

Canaan

An honor roll in granite is located on the common in the village center.

Candia

Candia's Soldiers' Monument lists the thirty-four Candia men who served along with Lieutenant William Herve Thomas, the town's only fatality. The memorial is located in front of the Fitts Museum.

Carroll

A plaque in granite honoring those who served in the Revolution and the First and Second World Wars, with a view of the mountains they left behind, is located on Twin Mountain, overlooking the intersection of Routes 3 and 302.

Center Barnstead

A World War I monument is part of a Civil War monument located in the town center.

Center Harbor

The Nichols Library, at the convergence of Plymouth and Main Streets and Meredith Road, has a granite slab with three bronze plaques featuring a World War I artillery battery in action, the emblems of three branches of the U.S. Armed Forces and the military badges of the Army, Air Force, Coast Guard, Marines and Navy. It was originally installed in 1920 to honor those who fought in the Civil War, the Spanish-American War and the First World War. It was expanded after the Second World War to include those veterans, and it was expanded again in 1992 to honor those who served in the Korean, Vietnam and Persian Gulf Wars.[44]

Charlestown

An honor roll was dedicated 1929 to those who served in "the World War." It is located at the intersection of Main Street and Depot Road.

Chester

A plaque in granite honors doughboys and one Red Cross nurse, Lillian McIntosh, in the town square on Main Street and Depot Road.

Claremont

A granite monument honoring the First and Second World Wars and the Korean and Vietnam Wars was dedicated in 1967 and spearheaded by the local Jaycee (Junior Chamber of Commerce) chapter and is located on north end of Broad Street Park.

Lacasse Park on North Street is named for the first Claremont man killed in the First World War. It was originally an island at the intersection of North, Broad and Washington Streets but was moved due to construction.

Colebrook/Stewartstown

An honor roll was dedicated in 1922 on the town green.

Concord

A memorial plaque dedicated to the 697 New Hampshire residents who died in World War I is located in the New Hampshire State House's Doric Hall.

There is a plaque dedicated to Brigadier General Charles Augustus Doyen, the commanding officer of the first regiment of Marines sent to France in June 1917. The Concord native died at Quantico, Virginia, on October 6, 1918. The monument was erected in 1919 by the City of Concord. The memorial is located at the intersection of North Main Street (U.S. 3) and Pitman Street and can be seen on the right when traveling east on North Main Street at the southeast corner of the original Merrimack County Superior Court. It was moved in 2018 from its previous location at the northwest corner of the court property to make way for a new building on the property.

Tribute plaque is located at Memorial Field, South Fruit Street.

Fletcher-Murphy Park on Fayette Street was renamed in memory of two nurses, Lucy Fletcher and Theresa Murphy, and was dedicated on November 11, 1937.

The American Legion Post 31 in Penacook is the host of a memorial.

Daniel Chester French gave his talent to his home state. In addition to the World War I monument in Exeter, he designed this tribute to the men from St. Paul's School and their sacrifice. *Michael Seamans, St. Paul's School.*

A plaque honoring Company M, the New Hampshire State Guard, can be seen in White's Park.

A memorial to Private Joseph Guyette, who died on June 15, 1918, in France, can be seen at Rolfe Park.

The Daniel Chester French sculpture is located in the St. Paul's School chapel.[45]

Derry

A plaque in granite listing the Champagne, Marne, Meuse-Argonne and other places Derry boys served can be found in MacGregor Park on East Broadway.

Dover

A monument erected by the City of Dover in memory of Lieutenant Donald W. Libby, who died in France on October 5, 1918, was dedicated in 1926 and can be reached through Arch Street.

An honor roll with three panels and 639 names is located in front of the municipal center.

The George Drouin memorial is located at the intersection of Portland Avenue and Chapel Street.

The Fabien Parent memorial is located at the intersection of Central Avenue and Chestnut Street.

A memorial to Private William H. Dobbins is located at the intersection of Broadway and St. Johns Street.

A Spanish-American War plaque is located in the municipal building.

Dublin

A plaque dedicated on September 15, 1918, can be found in Town Hall.

Dunbarton

A tablet set in stone is located in the town common.

Exeter

A memorial sculpted by Daniel Chester French stands in Gale Park.[46]

Enfield

A World War I monument is located on Route 4 near High Street in Veterans' Memorial Park.

Epsom

An honor roll for those who served in the First World War, Second World War and Korean War can be found on the town green.

Farmington

An honor roll dedicated in 1920 is located on Main Street.

Francestown

Francestown honors its veterans and casualties in the Great War with a monument at the Old Meeting House. The bronze relief plaque features a laurel branch and a scene of doughboys marching in formation with rifles over their shoulders. The plaque is set on the side of a granite boulder and was sculpted by Theo A.K. Kitson, who was paid $400. The monument was dedicated in 1920 at the junction of Routes 47 and 136.

Franconia Notch

A New Hampshire War Memorial was dedicated in 1928 on the I-93 Franconia Notch Parkway.

Franklin displays its Honor Roll for the First World War on its Soldiers Memorial Building, now used as the town hall. *Sheila Bailey.*

Franklin

A memorial to William A. Fenlason, Franklin's first casualty in the Great War, can be found at the intersection of Central and West Bow Streets.

Gilford

An honor roll plaque set in rock can be found on Potter Hill Road.

Goffstown

A plaque honoring 102 of the town's men who served in World War I is part of a war monument that was dedicated on June 16, 1916, to honor the Civil War. It was donated by Henry W. Parker and can be found in Monument Square.

Gorham

A World War I memorial features a fieldstone, concrete and stucco base and three bronze bas-relief plaques. The center plaque features a full-length female figure representing Liberty, and she is flanked by a World War I soldier and sailor. The other plaques feature images of eagles in flight.

The base has a concrete floor two steps above ground level, round fieldstone pillars and stucco walls above benches bearing the plaques. The base for a flagpole is a U-shaped projection with fieldstone sides and a concrete top. It was built by W.F. Kendall in 1922 to honor World War I veterans, and the plaques were later added on July 4, 1978. It features the inscription, "These gallant men of our armed forces have fought for the ideals which they know to be the ideals of our country." The sculpture can be found in Memorial Park at the convergence of Main, Park, Railroad and Glen Streets.

Greenville

A plaque set on granite with allegorical eagle relief also lists one nurse, Mary Drinan, who answered the call to serve. It was first dedicated on October 13, 1919, and then moved to Myrtle Marsh Memorial Veterans Park.

Groveton

A memorial dedicated in 1949 is located on the town square.

Hampstead

A plaque is located on the town green.

Hampton

An honor roll also honors two nurses, Jeannette P. White and Leonora B. Wing. An inscription reads, "When duty calls, Hampton is never found wanting." It was dedicated on November 12, 1919, with an all-day event.

The festivities started at 11:00 a.m. at the Lower Town Hall and included a banquet for the veterans at the Congregational church, a parade at 1:00 p.m. and the unveiling of the tablet at 2:30 p.m. It is located in front of the library and is mounted on a wall.[47]

Hanover

An obelisk stands in front of town hall.

Haverhill, North Haverhill and Pike

A plaque on granite includes Nurse Dorothy Morrell and was donated by the DAR in 1919. It is located on Dartmouth College Highway.

Hillsboro

A granite boulder with an honor roll and a bronze eagle with its wings spread on top was donated by Caroline A. Fox of Arlington, Massachusetts, and was fabricated by the T.F. McGann and Sons foundry. It honors the war dead from the Revolution to the First World War and was dedicated on August 24, 1930, at 29 School Street.

Hill

A square granite base is topped by an eagle with its talons resting on a small globe. This is the third eagle. The first was made of copper and then was replaced by one made of aluminum. The second was then replaced by the current eagle, which is removed and stored over the winter. There are honor roll plaques for those who served in the Civil War, the Spanish-American War and World War I. The sculpture was first installed in 1928 at 30 Crescent Street.

Holderness

Holderness has an all-wars honor roll, a bronze plaque on a granite boulder dated 1919. The World War I heroes are also listed on a granite monument honoring those who served in all American wars. A marker is located at the intersection of Daniel Webster Highway (U.S. 3) and New Hampshire Route 113 and can be seen on the left when traveling south on Daniel Webster Highway. The memorial is next to the public library.

Hooksett

A plaque on a rock honors Corporal George E. Merrill, who died on October 15, 1918, in the Argonne. He was buried in France. The monument was erected in 1933 by the American Legion and was originally located at the town hall but was moved to the memorial for soldiers of all wars on Jacob Square on the east side of the river next to the Congregational church.[48]

An honor roll plaque in Jacob Square mounted on granite blocks lists those who served and those who died in World War I.

Hopkinton

A granite boulder with a plaque accompanying other war memorials originally located near the front of town hall was moved ten years prior to this writing to the park along with several other monuments. It includes Nurse Laura Sanborn and is located in a triangular park in the center of Hopkinton Village, at the junction of Routes 202/9 and 103.

Hudson

Hudson sent seventy-one young men to serve in the Great War. In the March 1920 town meeting, the town voted to construct a memorial. This turned out to be a granite boulder with a bronze marker, and it was erected at Library Park. The total cost to the town was $977.65. The Dunklee Construction Co. was paid $647 to move the boulder into the park to place it on a foundation, the Hillsborough Granite Co. was paid $30 to cut and shape the boulder for the bronze tablet and the William Highton & Sons

Co. was paid $300 for the bronze tablet and for setting it into the stone. Three Hudson residents lost their lives in World War I: Leland H. Woods, Carlton L. Petry and Harold M. Spalding. They were memorialized on June 25, 1922, with three freshly planted trees with bronze markers at their bases also at Library Park. The trees were donated by the local chapter of the GAR, and the dedication ceremony was shared between the GAR and the Town of Hudson.

Jaffrey

The town is home to the *Buddies Monument*.[49]

Jefferson

A war monument was dedicated on September 22, 1922 (American Revolution, Civil War, Spanish-American War and World War I). It has a granite base, bronze reliefs and a full-length figure of a World War I soldier in uniform with a canteen, bayonet and rifle. The other reliefs are the seals of the United States and New Hampshire. Plaques were later added to honor those who served from the Revolution to World War II. It can be found on Route 2/Presidential Highway.

Kingston

A memorial was dedicated on May 30, 1924, on the town green, also called the Plains.

Laconia

A memorial honors those who served in World War I and the Spanish-American War in Veterans Square.

Lancaster

In Centennial Park on Main Street, a granite base holds a bronze eagle with its wings spread. It was cast by Gorham Silversmiths and was dedicated on Memorial Day in 1951. It pays tribute to those from Lancaster who served in the First and Second World Wars, with those who served in Korea and Vietnam added later.

Lebanon

A memorial plaque set in granite was installed in 1938 in Colburn Park.

Lempster

A memorial honor roll (World War I) was dedicated in 1920 in the town park on Lempster Street.

Lincoln

Bicentennial Memorial Park was dedicated on July 4, 1976, on Main Street.

Littleton

A memorial is located at the intersection of Main (New Hampshire Route 18) and Maple Streets and can be seen on the right when traveling west on Main Street.

Londonderry

A memorial granite slab has a bronze plaque and bas-relief of an eagle in flight. Below that is a relief of a World War I scene: an artillery squad with two cannons manned by soldiers and infantrymen with their guns ready. The slab is part of the honor roll of Londonderry in the town common.

Lyndeborough

A memorial was dedicated in 1926 at 126 Forest Road.

Madison

World War I memorial, part of a trifold with memorials to World War II and the Korean War, was installed by Silver Lake Women's Club on Village Road. A quote from the prophet Joel was included: "Tell your children of it and let your children tell their children, and their children another generation."

Manchester

Memorials to the war dead can be found in Victory Park, Kalivas Park, Harriman Park and Mount Calvary Cemetery.[50]

Lieutenant William Jutras

A plaque was dedicated to Lieutenant William Jutras, who served with the 103rd Infantry, 26th Division, and was killed in action on September 26, 1918, in Riaville, France, at the age of twenty-six. He received the Distinguished Service Cross posthumously for his actions. The American Legion on the West Side is also named for him. The plaque is located in McGregor Park on the corner of Amory and McGregor Streets.[51]

Henry J. Sweeney Park

Private Henry John Sweeney was the first man from Manchester to die in World War I. Sweeney was killed in action on February 13, 1918, in Soissons, France. His name is also listed on an American Legion post in Manchester. The park is located on South Main Street.[52]

Gossler Park and School

The park and school are named for Private Henry Gossler, who died on November 1, 1918, of wounds he received in the Argonne Forest. The school was dedicated on January 20, 1957.[53]

Herman F. Little Square

The square honors Private Herman F. Little, who died on July 20, 1918, in Chateau-Thierry, France.

Jeremiah Morley Plaque

Morley died on July 20, 1918, near Chateau-Thierry, and the plaque was dedicated on September 3, 1923. It was placed on the front of St. Patrick's Church.[54]

Stark Park

On May 20, 1922, Gold Star Mothers from the Henry J. Sweeney Post Auxiliary, state and city officials, clergy and veterans planted forty-seven trees on North River Road to represent the forty-seven Manchester lives lost in the Great War.

Marlborough

An honor roll on the town green includes an inscription from President Wilson's Thanksgiving proclamation: "In a righteous cause they have won immortal glory and have nobly served their nation in serving mankind."

Milford

A memorial dedicated in 1925 can be found in the town hall lobby.
   A memorial dedicated in 2005 can be seen on the Oval.

Nashua

Nashua built a temporary Victory Arch, which was displayed on Main Street from November 1918 to January 1920. It was erected to celebrate the original Armistice Day, marking the end of the First World War, and it remained in place until January 1920. The arch held the dates July 4, 1776, marking the birth of this country, and November 11, 1918, marking Armistice Day, and the years 1812, marking the War of 1812, and 1846, marking the Mexican-American War.

A World War I cannon is located in Greeley Park.

A flagpole was placed at city hall and dedicated to those who served in the Great War.

The town is home to the Deschenes Oval.[55]

Newington

A plaque on granite honors the Revolution, the War of 1812, the Mexican-American War, the Civil War and World War I. It was donated by the Shakespearean Club in 1926 and can be seen on Nimble Hill Road.

Newmarket

The town bandstand was dedicated in 1921 in honor of the World War I troops.

Newport

Newport honored its heroes of the Great War with a cast-iron honor roll erected by the Newport Board of Trade two months before the Armistice was signed. While townspeople wanted it relocated to a park, such as the town common, it remained in its Main Street location. It was reconditioned in 1928, with Delford R. Graves painting the background black, the names of the survivors in aluminum and the names of the dead in gold. It was later dismantled, with a high probability that it was used for scrap iron during the Second World War.[56]

North Conway/Conway

A plaque set in rock can be found at Schouler Park on Main Street. It displays the names of forty-six local residents who served in World War I. It includes two nurses, Dara M. Anderson and Edna L. Ricker.

A plaque can be seen at Conway Public Library.

The American Legion Post 46 on Tasker Hill Road in Conway was dedicated in memory of Ralph W. Shirley, the first Conway man killed in Europe during World War I. Shirley's name also appears at the top of a list of twelve names on East Conway Veterans Memorial near Sherman Farm.

An honor roll can be found in Veterans' Park on Mill Street and Route 302.

North Hampton

A plaque in rock honors veterans in front of the Stone Building, the original town library, now in the National Register of Historic Places. Erected in 1923 by Smalley, Hobbs and Hunter of Rochester, with the brass plaques by Albert Russell and Sons of Newburyport, Massachusetts. Two original plaques honor Civil War and World War I veterans.

Northfield

A plaque set in rock can be found at 18 Park Street near Hall Memorial Library.

Northumberland

A plaque on a rock with an eagle is one of four gray granite memorials dedicated to the residents who served in World War I, World War II and the Korean and Vietnam Wars. The original World War I monument was moved here from another location and was joined by a World War II monument and rededicated on January 1, 1949. Its original location was the junction of Church and State Streets, next to the library. It is now located on Route 3/Main Street near its junction with West Street.

Northwood

An honor roll with a plaque on a rock and an eagle can be seen in front of town hall.

Orford

An honor roll plaque set in stone includes one nurse, Hazel Dustin. It includes the inscription, "Erected in honor of those men and women of Orford who were in the service of the nation, the Allies and humanity during the years when the German armies attempted to conquer the civilizations of earth and failed." It is located on Dartmouth College Highway (New Hampshire Route 10), one-tenth of a mile north of Bridge Street (New Hampshire Route 25A). It can be seen on the left when traveling north.

Pittsburg

An honor roll mounted on a piece of granite is located in a town park near 1598 Daniel Webster Highway.

The bronze plaque features a woman wearing a hard hat and carrying a tool and the scroll on which the names of the twenty-nine men who served are inscribed.

A monument (World War I, World War II and Korean and Vietnam Wars) was dedicated in 1974 in Dustin Park.

Plainfield

A two-sided honor roll features the town's one casualty, Harry D. Thrasher, in gold. There were originally two World War I honor rolls, but only one has survived. It is located in front of Philip Read Memorial Library at 1088 Route 12-A.

The Harry Thrasher marker can be found at 62 Thrasher Road.[57]

Portsmouth

The town is home to the Memorial Bridge.[58]

The honor roll in Goodwin Park includes nine nurses.

A memorial at Portsmouth Plains comprises twenty-six cement posts, each holding a small plaque. There is also a boulder with a larger plaque. Each stone has the name of a deceased person and their rank and birth and death dates. It includes Army doctors, Army infantrymen, one nurse, two Marines, sailors and one sailor who, also with his ship, have never been found. It was sponsored by the Town of Portsmouth and dedicated in 1919.

A memorial to the Spanish-American War can be found in Goodwin Park on Islington Street.

A fountain near the entrance to Prescott Park was dedicated to Ensign Charles Emerson Hovey. Hovey, a native of Portsmouth, was killed in the Philippines in 1911. The portrait relief was made by F.W. Allen in 1918.

Raymond

A plaque is dedicated to Dudley Gilman Tucker and Emerson Maple in the Dudley Tucker Library. Tucker died near Soissons on July 8, 1918. Maple died in Chateau-Thierry on July 20, 1918.

Rindge

A plaque on a rock with a banner of victory and peace includes three nurses, Amy E. Hale, Alice W. Lyon and Mary E. Wellington. It is located at the entrance to the meetinghouse.

World War I veterans are also honored with a plaque at Rindge Memorial School, which was erected in 1952.

A model for *Ecce Homo* can be found in the Cathedral of the Pines.[59]

Rumney

A plaque on a rock shares a monument that recognizes the American Revolution, the War of 1812, the Mexican-American War, the Civil War and the Spanish-American War in Town Park.

Springfield

A freestanding honor roll can be found on the town green.

Sutton

A memorial roll can be found on the town common.

Temple

There is an honor roll in Town Park that is part of an overall veterans' memorial. The honor roll includes one nurse, Hattie T. Hayward.

Thornton

A plaque in rock in Town Park includes one nurse, Lillie Fifield.

Tilton

A plaque mounted in rock includes one nurse, Winifred Long. It includes a statement: "They served without thought of self that the principles of liberty, justice and loyalty might prevail for all mankind." It is located in Veterans Square and was dedicated in 1919.

Troy

A plaque on granite includes the inscription, "In honor of our boys of Troy, NH, 1927—The Great World War—1919, for liberty and humanity." The memorial can be found on Central Square just north of New Hampshire Highway 12 and can be seen on the left when traveling north.

Wakefield

A World War I plaque in the town common is set in granite and flanked by two "wings" featuring names from World War II. It includes one nurse, Margaret Blake, and was given by the Lowe family in 1960.

Warner

A plaque is part of an overall tribute to General Walter Harriman, who served in the Civil War and is an ancestor of Manchester's World War I hero Lynn Harriman. The Warner town meeting in 1921 voted to dedicate $1,000 to a Great War monument, and in 1922, the town voted to turn the money over to Post 39, which erected the plaque in town hall.

Webster

Five honor rolls to World War I, World War II, the Korean and Vietnam Wars and the "supreme sacrifice" are located at the intersection of Allen Road and Battle Street (Route 127).

Westmoreland

A plaque on a stone kiosk can be seen in the town common near the library and across from town hall.

Whitefield

A monument dedicated in 1944 includes two nurses, Anna M. Gove and Lorna L. Whitcher. It is located on the town green.

A granite trifold monument was built in 1994. World War II is featured on one side and World War I and the Korean and Vietnam Wars are featured on the other. It can be found in King Square in the town common.

Winchester

A plaque on granite can be found on the west side of town hall.

Wolfeboro

An honor roll lists the 110 from Wolfeboro who went to war, including the 3 who did not come back, marked with a star. It was dedicated in 1941 in front of Carpenter School.

Woodstock/North Woodstock

A freestanding stone monument in the shape of a shield was dedicated on May 30, 1921. It lists the twenty-five residents who served, including three casualties. It can be found in the triangular park on U.S. 3 (Daniel Webster Highway).

4

Paying the Price

The Second World War

The Great War was called "the war to end all wars." It was meant to "whup the Kaiser," but it set the stage for a worse tyrant, the slaughter of six million people and whatever innocence hadn't already been lost.

At the end of the First World War, the Allies were determined that such a conflict would never happen again. They aimed their lens of punishment toward Germany, which they held responsible for the four years of carnage. The Treaty of Versailles, hammered out at the Paris Peace Conference in 1919, punished Germany with several measures, including a demand for the financial restitution of $132 billion in gold marks, about $269 billion in today's currency. The German leaders who signed the Armistice on November 11, 1918, believed that Woodrow Wilson's "Fourteen Points" would form the basis of the treaty. They were wrong.

In addition to the reparations, which would take the country ninety-two years to pay, Germany was told to surrender 10 percent of its territory, conduct war crimes trials against Kaiser Wilhelm II, maintain a limited Army and Navy and not to maintain an Air Force. When the Great Depression gripped the world, ordinary Germans fell captive to radical political philosophies, setting the stage for Adolf Hitler and the Second World War. A small man with a loud voice and a ridiculous mustache fed Germany's longing for its old power with appeals to racial purity and superiority.

Hitler's invasion of Poland in 1939 plunged Europe into the Second World War. The United States took up arms after the Japanese bombing of Pearl

Harbor in 1941. And New Hampshire sent approximately ten thousand men and women to help the exhausted Allies.

It was the right thing to do. On the home front, scrap metal drives, war bond sales and victory gardens contributed to freedom's new cause. And another crop of heroes grew out of the rocky soil of New Hampshire. They included men like Manchester's Rene Gagnon.

When is a hero still a hero? Rene Gagnon was a fatherless boy who left school early, like many others, to take a job in a Manchester mill. He would have lived out his life in happy obscurity but for the Second World War and Iwo Jima. Gagnon enlisted and fought in the Pacific theater, gaining the rank of corporal. On February 23, 1945, he was identified as part of a group of servicemen, including four other Marines and a Navy corpsman, who put their shoulders into raising the American flag on Mount Suribachi in Iwo Jima. At the end of a thirty-six-day battle involving seventy thousand Marines and eighteen thousand Japanese soldiers, America wrested control of the island from Japan. The powerful image was captured by Associated Press photographer Joseph Rosenthal, and these men became heroes in a different way. Gagnon was summoned home for a bond tour, returned to the Pacific, served briefly in China and came home for good in 1945.

The photograph and its young subjects became "the stuff of legend, memorialized in books and film."[60] The boy from the mills was featured in *LIFE* magazine and had a cameo in John Wayne's *Sands of Iwo Jima* before settling down with his wife, Pauline, and young son, Rene Jr. He worked different jobs, battled alcoholism and eventually formed a travel agency with Pauline. Gagnon lived modestly and was humble about his place in history, but his friends stretching back to childhood wanted more, and in 1965, veterans' groups and hometown friends began the first of several fundraisers to make a monument. Gagnon died of a heart attack in 1979, before the monument could be finished. It was dedicated on May 29, 1995.

But it was war, and things were bound to get confused. In 2016, the Marine Corps released the first corrected identity: John Bradley was mistaken for PFC Harold Schulze of Detroit, one of the actual flagbearers. The Marine Corps declared on October 16, 2019, that Gagnon had been incorrectly identified as one of the flagbearers. When the first flag raised over Mount Suribachi was deemed too small, a second one was procured. Gagnon, a runner in the Fifth Marine Division, received a larger flag to take up the mountain. Corporal Harold "Pie" Keller was misidentified as Gagnon in the photograph.

John Clayton, a Manchester author and executive director of the Manchester Historic Association (MHA), has written about Gagnon and organized exhibits on Gagnon at his facility. Clayton grew up in the city and remembers being influenced by the "legend." "When I was growing up, my mother would point him out in parades," Clayton recalled. When the Marines released their bombshell in 2019, Clayton said he felt some disappointment, both personally and professionally. He and the staff had to rework all their Rene Gagnon material, including a script for an audio tour. He felt more disappointed in the Marines than in Gagnon, noting that he was surprised "that they continued to pursue this after seventy-five years." But Clayton and the MHA deal in facts, and they updated their materials.

Clayton is philosophical about the change. His own father didn't see combat, but he served on an aircraft carrier, guiding the planes in with ping-pong paddles. "He was," Clayton said, "a human crosshairs." And he was still a hero to his son. David Kenney, a retired Navy commander and chairman of the New Hampshire Veterans Advisory Committee, agrees. Quoted in Shawne Wickham's article in 2019 , he stated, "Anybody that was there, in my opinion, was a hero regardless of whether they were on the summit or not."[61]

The irony, Clayton said, is that Gagnon's hometown "moment in the sun" was taken from him. Manchester was set to honor him with a parade, but the celebration was canceled. "It was the day Franklin Roosevelt died," Clayton said.

But whatever really happened, Gagnon enlisted, he served and he was there. He carried the flag, both literally and figuratively. Gagnon's monument is located in Victory Park in Manchester, a stone's throw from the massive World War I tribute.

Manchester's Greatest Generation included men like Dr. Ben Richard Bronstein. A lieutenant with the U.S. Medical Corps, Bronstein was the first naval officer from New Hampshire to give his life in World War II. He was lost in action aboard the destroyer the USS *Jacob Jones* on February 28, 1942. Bronstein's hometown honored him with a 2.4-acre park at the junction of Hanover and Beech Streets. The park, formerly known as Hanover Square, also features a statue honoring veterans of the Spanish-American War, the War with the Philippines and the Boxer Rebellion. He is also honored with two ships named after him, the USS *Bronstein* (DD 189), which was launched on November 14, 1943, and the USS *Bronstein* (DD 1037), which was commissioned in 1963.

Manchester's official World War II monument saw two dedications. The World War II memorial was first dedicated on September 9, 1944, and featured 8,517 names. To a crowd of 15,000, then-mayor Joseph T. Benoit said that the eight-sided structure was temporary. It looked permanent

Manchester's Rene Gagnon was still a hero—just not the hero people thought he was. *Sheila Bailey*.

Dr. Ben Richard Bronstein's home city of Manchester honored him with a park that bears his name. *Sheila Bailey*.

The proud Manchester citizens dedicated this World War II memorial twice. *Sheila Bailey.*

enough, placed on a concrete foundation with plywood panels under glass and room for 10,000 names. Names were added as the war raged on. The elements wreaked havoc with the monument, and it was dismantled in 1958. But the people of Manchester remembered their heroes and dedicated a replica of the first monument in 2009. The park was originally intended to honor veterans of the Civil War, and a large and ornate memorial can be found there.[62] But Manchester eventually expanded the park's purpose to honor all veterans of all of America's armed conflicts. Veterans Park also includes engraved benches and the *Battlefield Cross* installation, which was sponsored by the New Hampshire Disabled American Veterans.

The Allies used everything they could to outwit Hitler and Mussolini, from children's scrap metal drives to soldiers on skis. The Tenth Mountain Division trained troops to work in high and cold terrain. The Tenth included many New Englanders who had grown up skiing, though most of their training took place in the West. A group did train briefly in Lincoln, New Hampshire, in 1942. The Eighty-Seventh Mountain Infantry, a detachment of the Tenth, taught hiking and mountaineering techniques to soldiers from

The Tenth Mountain Division trained briefly in the New Hampshire mountains and is honored with this monument on top of Mount Washington. *Patrick Hummel, Department of Natural and Cultural Resources, State of New Hampshire.*

Texas and Oklahoma. Instructors from Fort Lewis, Washington, instructed the southerners on rappelling and belaying in Franconia Notch on Cannon Mountain below the Old Man of the Mountains. The men selected for the Tenth had their own special cold-weather gear, including an insulated glove with an open spot for pulling a trigger. They are memorialized with a plaque on the top of Mount Washington.

And Concord had a built-in venue to honor its boys: the statehouse plaza. A granite monument honors the men—and by now, several women, who took up arms, telephones, typewriters or bandages.

New Hampshire's native sons gave the state plenty to be proud of, and no town was prouder than Pittsfield. General Harrison Thyng, technically a native of Barnstead, served with distinction in the Pacific, North African and European theaters of the Second World War, flying 162 missions, downing 5 enemy planes and at least once being caught behind enemy lines.[63]

Thyng attended a one-room schoolhouse in Barnstead. At Pittsfield High School, he was a standout athlete, lettering in three sports. He graduated from the University of New Hampshire in 1939 with a pre-law degree and an ROTC commission as a second lieutenant. He then joined the Army Air Corps and learned to fly. Thyng was promoted to captain

Concord's World War II memorial is part of this granite trifold on the statehouse plaza. *Sheila Bailey.*

and then major and served in England, flying combat missions. He flew British Spitfires and was credited with 162 combat sorties, with 5 enemy planes destroyed. He also served in North Africa. He was promoted to full colonel at the age of twenty-six, returned home briefly and then deployed to the Pacific, where he led a group conducting dive-bombing and strafing raids on targets in Japan and China.

After the war, Thyng served as an instructor with the National Guard and was instrumental in the forming of the National Guard in Maine, New Hampshire and Vermont. But his country still needed him on the front lines, and in October 1951, Thyng deployed to Korea, where he served in the Korean Conflict. He flew 114 missions in Korea and holds the distinction—with only five others—of being one of the few "flying aces" to fly missions with both propeller planes and jet aircraft.

Thyng founded the New England Aeronautical Institute in Nashua, which later became Daniel Webster College, and he worked and consulted for the Air Defense Command and NORAD. The only thing he ever publicly failed at was a Senate candidacy in 1966. His monument was erected by the Pittsfield Historical Society on July 17, 2004.

Above: Harrison Thyng, the boy colonel and a flying ace in two wars, is honored by his adopted hometown of Pittsfield. *Sheila Bailey.*

Opposite, top: Portsmouth's Russell Hanscom gave his life for his country at the age of twenty-one. *Sheila Bailey.*

Opposite, bottom: This monument in Nashua's Railroad Square honors members of every branch of service, both men and women, who served in the Second World War. *Sheila Bailey.*

Other young men never knew what they could have become, like Portsmouth's Russell Hanscom, who died in Europe at the age of twenty-one. Hanscom was a private first class with Company M, Fifteenth Infantry, Third Infantry Division of the U.S. Army. He was killed in action in Italy and was awarded the Purple Heart posthumously. Russell Hanscom's memorial was dedicated on November 11, 1956, and rededicated on November 11, 2000. It is located on Kearsarge Way in his hometown. His memorial was sponsored by the Frank E. Booma American Legion Post.

Nashua wasn't taking any chances in the war that soaked up the best and the brightest. It honors members of every branch of service, both men and women, in the monument at the Deschenes Oval in Railroad Square. Though the "war to end all wars" didn't live up to this title, Nashua

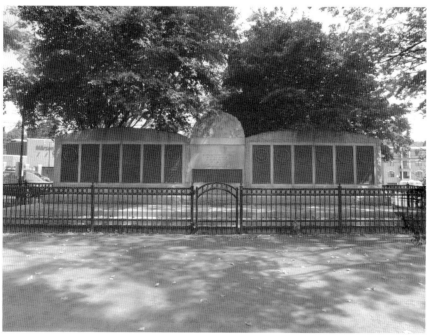

```
EAB V UNE INA 02/07   OP   OP
T SELF

FROM 9 T.C.C. (FWD)     070557B
TO 50TH TCW AND GPS
   52ND TCW AND GPS
   53RD TCW AND GPS
   9TH TROOP CARRIER SERVICE WING

FROM SHAEF (FWD)     070410B
TO------
INFO----

CONFIDENTIAL  QHR  BT

FWD 20801  CONFIDENTIAL
BOOK MESSAGE
--------------
PARA ONE.PD A REPRESENTATIVE OF THE GERMAN HIGH COMMAND SIGNED
THE UNCONDITIONAL PAREN FROM SHAEF FORWARD SIGNED EISENHOWER
CITE  SHGCT UNPAREN S U R R E N D E R OF ALL GERMAN LAND CMA
SEA CMA AND AIR FORCES IN EUROPE TO THE ALLIED EXPEDITIONARY FORCE
AND SIMULTANEOUSLY TO THE SOVIET HIGH COMMAND AT ZERO ONE FOUR
ONE HOURS CENTRAL EUROPEAN TIME CMA SEVEN MAY UNDER WHICH ALL
FORCES WILL CEASE ACTIVE OPERATIONS AT ZERO ZERO ZERO ONE BAKER
HOURS  NINE MAY PD PARA TWO EFFECTIVE IMMEDIATELY ALL OFFENSIVE
OPERATIONS BE ALLIED EXPEDITIONARY FORCE WILL CEASE AND TROOPS
WILL REMAIN IN PRESENT POSITIONS PD MOVES INVOLVED
IN OCCUPATIONAL DUTIES WILL CONTINUE PD DUE TO DIFFICULTIES OF
COMMUNICATION THERE MAY BE SOME DELAY IN SIMILAR ORDERS
REACHING ENEMY TROOPS SO FULL DEFENSIVE PRECAUTIONS WILL BE
TAKEN PD PARA THREE PD ALL INFORMED DOWN TO AND INCLUDING
DIVISIONS CMA TACTICAL AIR COMMANDS AND GROUPS CMA BASE SECTIONS
CMA AND EQUIVALENT PD NO REPEAT NO RELEASE WILL BE MADE
TO THE PRESS PENDING AN ANNOUNCEMENT BY THE HEADS OF THE THREE
GOVERNMENTS PD

BT 07/0410B
BT 07/0507B
WB  BBB
```

The authors' father and grandfather saved this announcement of the cessation of hostilities.
Kathleen D. Bailey.

continues to honor the memory of its sons and daughters who picked up where Amedee Deschenes had to leave off.

The so-called Greatest Generation came home, and most of them didn't talk about the war. This book's authors' father/grandfather served. He didn't see combat—he worked as a codebreaker—but he didn't even talk about that. He never joined the VFW or the American Legion, and he never squeezed into his old uniform to march in parades. But when the authors went through his things, they found he had saved everything: news clippings, enlistment papers, memos, photographs—and the message that came over the wire announcing victory in Europe.

They knew what they were doing, and they did it.

Listings: World War II

Acworth

A tribute can be found in Memorial Park.

Alstead

Alstead's World War I and World War II monuments were donated by the American Legion Britton-Porter Post and Veterans of Foreign Wars Whiton-Pelton Posts and dedicated on August 14, 1949. They were destroyed by the October 2005 flood, and the town rebuilt these monuments along with monuments to the Korean, Vietnam and post-Vietnam wars. They were dedicated in 2008 in the town center.

Amherst

A plaque can be found in the town common.

Antrim

Memorial Park is located on Jameson Avenue and holds Antrim's tribute.

Atkinson

World War II and the Korean War are memorialized on a plaque on a rock in Dow Common.

Auburn

A memorial is located on the town green.

Bath

A granite monument can be found in the village center.

Berlin

A World War II plaque in rock can be found in Veterans Park, which was established on November 11, 2006.

Bethlehem

A plaque on a rock includes two nurses, Margaret C. Conley and Muriel E. Winterbottom. It is located on the town green on Route 302.

Brookline

A granite monument with engraved names can be found at town hall.

Charlestown

A granite monument honors World War II and the Korean War on Route 12 in front of town hall and can be seen on the left when traveling north on Main Street.

Chesterfield

A monument can be found in the center of Chesterfield on Old Chesterfield Road, opposite from the school, behind the Chesterfield Historical Society and in front of the American Legion Hall.

Concord

A granite trifold memorial (World War II, Korean War and Vietnam War) was dedicated on November 11, 1953, at the statehouse on Main Street.[64]

Derry

A memorial (World War II) can be found in MacGregor Park on East Broadway.

Dover

A granite memorial includes an inscription: "A tribute to the finest America has to offer, the Citizen Soldier, then, now, and forever. 1940–1946." The memorial is located at the intersection of Washington Street and Henry Law Avenue and can be seen on the left on Washington Street. It is located within Henry Law Park.

The town is home to the Maurice J. Burke memorial. Burke was watertender first class on the destroyer *Maddox* and was lost in action on July 11, 1943. The memorial can be found at the intersection of Central and Hanson Streets.

Dublin

The Memorial Honor Roll (World War II) was dedicated in 1947 on Main Street at Town Hall.

Effingham

An honor roll is located at the intersection of Route 113 South from Route 25 and Plantation Road.

Enfield

A World War II monument is located on Route 4 near High Street in Veterans Memorial Park.

Epsom

An honor roll donated by the Elwood Wells American Legion is located at the American Legion on Short Falls Road.

A tank and machine gun given by the American Legion can also be seen at the American Legion on Short Falls Road.

Exeter

A cannon designed by Exeter resident George Leonard Smith was donated by Smith to his town after World War II.

A granite war memorial displaying symbols of branches of service can be seen in front of the town office building, Front Street.

Two stones were erected in 1964 as memorials to World War II, the Korean War and later the Vietnam War. They are next to a boulder and plaque dedicated to General Gilman Marston, a Civil War veteran, in Exeter Cemetery at the Arbor Street entrance.

Farmington

A memorial (World War II and the Korean and Vietnam Wars) is located at the Clarence L. Perkins American Legion Post on Main Street and was dedicated in 1955.

Francestown

A plaque on the rock supporting the town bandstand can be seen in the town square.

Franklin

There is a plaque on a rock that also memorializes the Korean and Vietnam Wars at city hall.

The Wall of Heroes inside City Hall is a display of those who served.

Fremont

A granite slab with plaques can be seen on the town hall lawn and was dedicated in 1951.

Gorham

The Nineteenth Mountain Division Memorial's (World War II) plaque reads: "Dedicated by the New England Chapter of the 10th Mountain Division in memory of comrades who gave their lives in the Aleutians and Italy in WWII." On skis and snowshoes, the Nineteenth Mountain Division spearheaded the Fifth Army to shatter the German defenses in Italy. The monument is located on the Mount Washington summit.[65]

A granite monument with "wings" on either side honors World War I and World War II and the Korean, Vietnam, Lebanon and Grenada, Panama and Persian Gulf Wars. It is located in the town common.

Goshen

There is a memorial to World War II and the Korean and Vietnam Wars that was erected by the town in 1975 in the town park.

Grafton

There is a plaque in a rock in Town Park.

Groveton

Camp Stark (a World War II POW camp) held approximately 250 German and Austrian soldiers, most of whom were captured in North Africa and Normandy. They lived in Camp Stark while working in the forest cutting pulpwood, which was vital to wartime industry. The camp was a remodeled Civilian Conservation Corps (CCC) camp. The camp was opened in 1944 and closed in the spring of 1946, when the prisoners of war were returned to their homeland. Its marker is located on Stark Highway (New Hampshire Route 110) eight and a half miles east of U.S. 3. It can be seen on the right when traveling east.[66]

Hampton

The Memorial Honor Roll (World War II) is located at the courthouse.

Hancock

A memorial (World War II and the Korean and Vietnam Wars) was dedicated on August 16, 2003, and located at the Pine Ridge Cemetery.

A plaque can be seen on the village green.

Hanover

A granite monument is located at the intersection of Lebanon and Summer Streets and can be seen on the left when traveling west on Lebanon Street. It is located in front of Hanover High School.

Henniker

A plaque on a rock was dedicated in May 1949. It is located in Woodman Park in front of town hall.

A memorial flagpole was installed at 41 Lebanon Street.

Hill

Veterans Park honors veterans of all wars.

Hooksett

There is a monument (World War II) in Jacob Square. Jacob Square is itself named for a Hooksett soldier, Private Robert T. Jacob, who was killed in action in Italy on November 28, 1943, and was buried in the nearby Holy Rosary Cemetery. The monument includes the names of all Hooksett men who served in the Second World War. The granite was quarried from a local quarry. Two urns bear the names of Private Omer Nadeau (MIA, 1945) and Marine corporal Raymond Follansbee (KIA, 1943). The park also includes tributes to prisoners of war and Gold Star mothers.[67]

Jacob Square, Hooksett, is the town's veterans park and is named for Private Robert T. Jacob, who died on November 28, 1943, in Italy. *Sheila Bailey.*

Hopkinton

A plaque on a rock (World War II and the Korean and Vietnam Wars) is located in the triangular park in the village center.

Hudson

A granite memorial honoring all wars (World War I, World War II and the Korean, Vietnam, Beirut, Panama, Grenada, Persian Gulf, Iraq and Afghanistan Wars) was donated by American Legion Post 48. It replaced the original World War II monument that was erected in 1942 in Library Park.

Jackson

A plaque on a rock can be viewed in Town Park.

Jaffrey

There is a Gold Star mothers monument in town square on Main Street.

Keene

Cheshire County's veterans memorial comprises a plaque on a rock that was dedicated on May 30, 1988, at 10 Central Square.

The park in Central Square has stone benches that were donated by veterans' organizations and trees planted by the Keene High School class of 1940 to honor their fallen classmates.

Kingston

A monument was dedicated on August 10, 1946, and was donated by Ruth and Arthur Reynolds. It is located on the town green, or the Plains.

Laconia

A trifold granite monument recognizes those who served in World War II and the Korean and Vietnam Wars in Veterans Square.

Lebanon

An honor roll is located in West Lebanon Cemetery.

Lempster

There is a plaque on a rock that was dedicated in 1947 and rededicated in 2018. It is located in front of Lempster Meetinghouse.

Lincoln

Plaques on a rock recognize those who served in World War I, World War II and the Korean, Vietnam, Grenada, Lebanon, Panama and Persian Gulf Wars. They are located in Bicentennial Memorial Park and were dedicated on July 4, 1976.

Londonderry

A threefold granite monument (World War II and the Korean and Vietnam Wars) was dedicated on August 15, 1988, in the town common.

Lyme

A single piece of granite honors the Spanish-American War, World War I and World War II in the town green.

Lyndeborough

A plaque can be seen on the green near town hall.

Madison

World War II is part of a trifold monument on Route 113, near a Baptist church, that also honors the Korean War.

Manchester

There is a memorial to Lieutenant Dr. Ben Richard Bronstein (World War II) in Bronstein Park.[68]

A memorial to Private First Class Rene Gagnon, an Iwo Jima flag raiser (World War II), is located in Victory Park.[69]

The town is home to the Merci Boxcar, a boxcar full of gifts and mementoes that was sent by a grateful French nation after World War II.[70]

A monument (World War II) that was dedicated in 2009 is located in Veterans Memorial Park.[71]

Veterans Park is also home to POW/MIA tributes, Korean War and Vietnam War tributes and the city's Civil War monument.[72]

Veterans Park also features several *Battlefield Crosses*, which were sponsored by the New Hampshire Disabled American Veterans (DAV. The crosses are made of a rifle with a fixed bayonet, symbolizing the fallen soldier; a pair of boots, symbolizing their final march; and a helmet and dog tags, neither of which is needed any more. It is the "price of freedom," according to the DAV.

Francis P. "Pat" Lally's memorial plaque can be found on South Main Street. Lally died when his escort carrier *Liscombe Bay* was torpedoed off the Gilbert Islands on November 23, 1943.[73]

The Robert W. Lewis Square, on the corner of Massabesic Street and Mammoth Road, was named for Lewis, who was killed in a bomber crash on November 2, 1942. It was dedicated on November 12, 1949.[74]

Meredith

The World War II Honor Roll comprises three panels of inscribed names, with four starred names, indicating they gave their lives in the conflict. The memorial is located on Main Street on the left side of the Meredith Public Library.

Merrimack

A memorial dedicated in 1991 can be found in Veterans Memorial Park on Camp Sargent Road.

Milford

Thirteen arborvitae trees commemorate the lives of the thirteen men from Milford who were killed in World War II, and they form a background for the fountain. Memorial Park (World War II) was dedicated in 1947 and is located on the southern side of the Union Square.[75]

A trifold monument honoring World War II and the Korean War can be found on the town common.

Milford pays tribute to its World War II losses with thirteen trees that were planted in Union Square. The park in Union Square is shown here in 1968. *Milford Historical Society.*

Milton

The World War II Honor Roll can be found in Veterans Memorial Park.

Newfields

A memorial (World War II) is located on Main Street.

Newington

A monument (World War II) was dedicated in 1949 on Nimble Hill Road, just south of the town library. It was sponsored by the Newington Veterans Association. There is also a plaque for the Korean War with no date on Nimble Hill Road, just south of town library.

Newport

On the town common is a granite slab with the names of the Newporters who were lost in World War II and the Korean, Vietnam and Gulf Wars.[76]

North Conway/Conway

An honor roll in granite is located in Schouler Park.

An honor roll can be found at Memorial Hospital, honoring the medical personnel who served their country.

Veterans Park is located at the intersection of Routes 16 and 302.

The honor roll at Kennett Middle School was originally placed in 1943 at the information booth and was replaced in 1997.

North Woodstock

A memorial (World War II) can be found in Soldiers Park.

The B-18 Bomber Memorial is located on Lost River Road.

Northwood

The Memorial Honor Roll (World War II) is located at 818 First New Hampshire Turnpike.

Orford

There is a memorial located on the town common.

Pittsfield

A monument (World War I, World War II and Korean and Vietnam Wars) was dedicated on May 30, 1975, in Dustin Park.

The Thyng Memorial (World War II and Korea) is located here.[77]

Portsmouth

The Russell A. Hanscom Memorial (World War II) on Kearsage Way was dedicated on November 11, 1956, and rededicated on November 11, 2000.[78]

The Portsmouth High School class of 1940's memorial (World War II) is located at 175 Parrott Avenue.

Raymond

A monument to those who served in World War II and Korea was dedicated on Memorial Day in 1984. A monument to those who served in Vietnam was dedicated in July 1984. They are located on the rim of a bandstand in the town common.

Rindge

The Cathedral of the Pines is located here.[79]

Rochester

A monument to all wars is located in Town Park.

A POW/MIA monument was established by the Rochester Veterans Council on November 11, 2004, in Town Park.

Rumney

A plaque on granite honoring World War II and the Korean and Vietnam Wars is located in the town common.

Tamworth

A trifold granite monument recognizes those who served in World War II and the Korean, Vietnam, Lebanon and Panama Wars. It was dedicated on August 12, 2007, in Veterans Park.

Temple

A granite monument to honor those who served in all American wars, including World War I; World War II; the Korean, Vietnam and Persian Gulf Wars; the Cold War and peacekeeping missions is located in the town green.

Tilton

The Tilton-Northfield Monument was dedicated in 1953 on the front lawn of Winnisquam High School.

Thornton

An honor roll plaque in a rock can be found in town park.

Troy

A granite monument to honor those who served in World War II, Korea and Vietnam is located on Central Square just south of Mill Street and can be seen on the left when traveling north.

Whitefield

A granite trifold monument was built in 1994. World War II is featured on one side, and World War I and the Korean and Vietnam Wars are featured on the other. It can be found in King Square in the town common.

Winchester

A trifold monument in granite honors those who served in World War II, Korea, Vietnam and "special conflicts." It was dedicated by the town in 1984 and is located on Main Street at town hall.

Wolfeboro

Plaques on granite honor those who served in World War II, Korea and Vietnam. They were dedicated on November 11, 1976, on Main Street.

Wolfeboro's Roll of Honor remembers those who served in World War II, the Korean War and the Vietnam War. *Sheila Bailey*.

5

The Shape of Things to Come

The Korean War

*I*t was the silent war, and it morphed into the forgotten war. The first war America fought in the East ended exactly where it started, with a divided nation and no real winner.

Since the beginning of the twentieth century, Korea had been a part of the Japanese Empire. After Japan's defeat in the Second World War, the decision of what to do with this ancient civilization fell to America and Russia. In August 1945, the peninsula was divided along the soon-to-be-famous thirty-eighth parallel. America took the southern half, and Russia took the northern half.

In the south, Syngman Rhee, an opponent of communism, established a dictatorship. In the north, Kim Il Sung was the communist dictator. Border skirmishes were common, with ten thousand men from both sides killed before the war was even declared.

But when the war was declared on June 25, 1950, seventy-five thousand soldiers from the North Korean People's Army poured across the thirty-eighth parallel, attacking the pro-West south. By July, American troops had entered the war on South Korea's side. The rationale from American officials was that the troops were sent to stop the spread of communism. President Harry Truman stated, "If we let Korea down, the Soviets will keep right on going and swallow up one place after another."

The war from the south was largely defensive until the end of the summer. Then Truman and General Douglas MacArthur decided that the war would liberate the north from the communists, and it became an offensive war.

MacArthur went even further, wanting to attack China, but Truman didn't want a war with China, even after Mao Zedong sent troops to North Korea. Truman eventually fired MacArthur.

The war reached a stalemate, and both states were willing to accept a ceasefire, with two separate countries divided at the thirty-eighth parallel. The two states differed sharply over the idea of POWs' forced repatriation, but they finally came to an agreement and signed an armistice on July 27, 1953, giving South Korea another 1,500 square miles and creating a 2-mile "demilitarized zone," or DMZ.

The United States retains, to this day, a presence in South Korea to carry out the Republic of Korea–United States Mutual Defense Treaty. Tensions existed between the two countries and resulted in several border skirmishes over the years. North Korea developed a nuclear missile capacity and isolated its people from the West.

In the twenty-first century, relations thawed, and the two countries began to talk, resulting in the Panmunjom Declaration on April 27, 2018.

Private First Class Roger B. Cote was the first Manchester man to die in the Korean Conflict. He was born on August 4, 1930, and died on September 1, 1950, in action near Masan in South Korea. Cote was the fourth of nine children and enjoyed playing the guitar and singing. He was seventeen years old when he joined the Army, signed for by his father, William, who was himself a veteran of World War I. Cote had completed his tour of duty, but it was extended, and he went to South Korea as part of the Eighth Field Artillery Battalion, Twenty-Fifth Infantry. He was killed in action when he received a machine gun bullet to the head. He was twenty years old.

The square at the corner of Valley and Massabesic Streets in Manchester was named in his honor at a ceremony on June 17, 1951. Hundreds of residents turned out for the dedication, and dozens of veterans' groups and governmental entities were represented. Cote was posthumously awarded the Purple Heart, the Korean Service Medal, the United Nations Service Medal, the National Defense Service Medal, the Korean Presidential Unit Citation and the Republic of Korea War Service Medal.[80]

Korean War veteran Maurice Mailhot, ninety-one, didn't just honor his own lost comrades. He was determined that his North Country neighbors not only remember the sacrifices their men and women made but also remember them in an orderly and organized fashion. Mailhot was concerned that Berlin's war monuments were "all mixed up," in no particular order and, in some cases, scattered all over the city.

Roger Cote Square is named for a Manchester man who lost his life in Korea. It is located at the junction of Valley and Massabesic Streets. *Sheila Bailey*.

Residents and veterans' organizations complained about political rallies being held near the monuments and children climbing on them. Mailhot, a lifetime member of VFW Post 2520, was appointed to oversee the realignment of monuments in Veterans Memorial Park on Glen Avenue in the North Country's largest city.

Mailhot and fellow committee member Peter McGillen moved the city's Civil War monument from its spot near a gazebo, placing it behind a new sign that was designed and donated by Mailhot. The World War II monument was shifted fourteen feet to accommodate the Spanish-American War monument, which was moved from the community field to Veterans Park. "That one was seventeen tons," Mailhot recalled in a phone interview, his voice clear and his memory sharp. "When it was first brought in, it was stuck on the east side—that was as far as the oxen could pull it." But that was before the invention of the backhoe, and modern equipment brought the tribute to the Spanish-American War veterans into Veterans Park. The World War I monument was more fragile, Mailhot remembered, and the decision was made to leave that one in Grand Trunk Park. But he made sure visitors to the park knew where it was, with another sign he designed and placed between the Spanish-American War and World War II monuments.

Mailhot did much of the landscaping himself. The park was rededicated on May 30, 2021.

Mailhot, also the recipient of two Purple Hearts, was honored by U.S. Senator Maggie Hassan as "Granite Stater of the Month" in June 2021. Hassan wrote in her commendation, "Long after his brave service to our country, Maurice continues to serve his community and has gone to extraordinary lengths to honor his fellow veterans." Mailhot was a volunteer, not a draftee. Inspired by an uncle's service in World War II, he volunteered for the regular Army on April 3, 1950. After basic training, he volunteered for the Airborne Rangers, an elite group of paratroopers, and when the Korean Conflict broke out, he volunteered to serve.

Most Americans know about the Korean Conflict through the television show *M*A*S*H*, and Mailhot said that is about 80 percent accurate. "But they always add a little bit," he said. But for all of Mailhot's work to recognize veterans, his own field of service remains relatively unfeted. The Korean Conflict's returnees did not come home to tickertape parades, flag-waving toddlers or sailors kissing nurses. They just came home, he said. "We blended in with the crowd." Jobs were scarce, Mailhot remembered, but he was able to get his old position back with a wholesale company. Though he built a life for himself, he did not see "his" war celebrated until he was a grandfather. "The Boy Scouts put up a Korean War memorial here in Berlin," he said. "My grandson was one of them. It was an Eagle project."

Mailhot thinks Korea wasn't well represented, in part, because nobody "won." It ended the way it began. And he thinks Vietnam veterans were underrepresented in the memorial department for years because the topic

Left: Maurice Mailhot of Berlin was a young army ranger when he fought in the Korean Conflict. He is shown here in 1951. *Maurice Mailhot.*

Above: Maurice Mailhot was the driving force behind the recent reorganization of the Veterans' Park in Berlin. He designed this sign, designed the new configuration and put in physical labor to make it happen. *Maurice Mailhot.*

was so touchy. But he's glad to see all veterans get their due in the redesigned Berlin park. "When I drive by, I think of all the people who were in all the wars," he mused. "They are not forgotten." While Mailhot likes to see others honored, he's laconic about his own service. "I got wounded twice and came out pretty good," he said. "I got no complaints. The state gives a free car registration to people with Purple Hearts."

Concord paid tribute to its Korean heroes with the Manchester Street Bridge. The old Manchester Street Bridge spanned the Merrimack River at Manchester Street, or U.S. Route 3. It was built in 1933, replacing an earlier wooden bridge, and in its time, it was the longest through truss bridge in New Hampshire. Built by the Lackawanna Steel Construction Corporation, it served the city until 1998, when it was replaced with the current bridge, which was dedicated to Korea's survivors and casualties. A twin bridge over the Merrimack on the Loudon Road end honors those who served in World War II.

Jack Barnes, now of Raymond, built a career as the owner of a chain of McDonald's restaurants, first in Massachusetts, then in New Hampshire, and had a second career that took him to the New Hampshire State House as a Senate majority leader. But in 1951, he was a college freshman, intent on preserving the same democracy for which his father had fought in World War I. He dropped out of college and enlisted in the Army. "My

This bridge over the Merrimack River at Manchester Street in Concord was completed in 1933. *Library of Congress, Historic Engineering Record.*

The Manchester Street Bridge over the Merrimack River was replaced in 1998 and dedicated to those who served in the Korean Conflict. A twin bridge over the Merrimack at Loudon Road is dedicated to Concord's participation in World War II. *Sheila Bailey.*

dad always told me, 'A country worth living in is a country worth fighting for.'" The younger Barnes was determined to "keep the communists out of America."

The first thing Barnes noticed about Korea was that "there were no toilet seats. I missed that, and I missed ice cream," Barnes said, only half-jokingly. But he quickly got the hang of life in a war zone after he spent the night on the floor of a tent in the relocation center. When a hand grabbed his foot, the young Barnes grabbed his rifle and aimed it. "I thought the Chinese were coming," he recalled. The offender turned out to be the center's chaplain, who wanted the new arrivals out so he could hold chapel in the tent.

Barnes also quickly learned the realities of war. He remembers trying to defend a certain hill with six other men. "Two of them were killed, two lived, including me, and two were never found." While the chaplain at the relocation center left him cold, the experience of actual war awakened the teenager's spirituality. Barnes later recalled, "I survived, and I knew my name was written in the book." He spent eleven months in Korea and was wounded once. After his tour, he came home on furlough before accepting a stateside assignment. He recalled looking at his parents, "and I thought they'd aged thirty years." His mother in particular "ran her hands all over me to make sure I was all right."

Both of Barnes's parents had plans for him to be grand marshal of the 1952 Winchester, Massachusetts Memorial Day Parade. The young soldier wasn't having any of it. "Then my dad said, 'Come on down to the Legion Hall, and I'll buy you a beer.'" Over the beers, the senior Barnes informed his son that a childhood friend of his, Billy Violetti, had been killed in Korea. "I didn't want you to know while you were over there," the older man told his son. The news hit the young soldier hard. "Billy was a friend of mine," he recalled. "We used to play war games around the hills of Winchester. I joined the Army; he joined the Marines." But the irony was yet to come, as the younger Barnes learned, "He was on the same ridge line I was on when he was killed."

Billy Violetti was the only Winchester man killed in the Korean Conflict, and his childhood friend laid the wreath on his grave. Barnes, a longtime town and state official, made sure no sacrifice was forgotten. He was instrumental in having a POW/MIA flag flown at the New Hampshire State House and a chaplain's flag was flown outside of the House of Representatives, donated by a friend in Raymond, Cal Warburton. He still remembers the two young men he served beside, one from Texas and one from Oklahoma, who were never accounted for.

Raymond resident Jack Barnes remembers the losses in the Korean Conflict and other wars at this bandstand in Raymond. *Sheila Bailey*.

Though Barnes and his fellow Korea veterans never sought attention, Barnes is pleased that his childhood home has erected a large memorial with Violetti's name on it and also his own. He's also proud of his adopted hometown of Raymond, with its honor rolls on the town common. "The town of Raymond," he said, "has done a tremendous job."

But like those in the Greatest Generation before them, the veterans of the Korean War weren't looking for applause. "When I came home on furlough, people would ask me, 'Hey, where you been?'" Barnes recalled with a chuckle. "It didn't bother me. I wasn't looking for recognition."

The Korean Conflict was short and bloody. Even as peace talks hashed out the details, the groundwork was being laid in French Indochina for a longer and equally bloody war that would divide America, shake it to its core and reassemble it as something no one recognized.

Listings: The Korean War

Acworth

A tribute can be found in Memorial Park.

Alstead

A plaque on a rock was dedicated in 2008 and was donated by Alstead's veterans in the town center.

Amherst

The Korean War, along with the Spanish-American War, the Mexican Border Conflict and the Vietnam War, was recognized with a monument erected on the town green by the historical society in 1985.

Antrim

Memorial Park is located on Jameson Avenue.

Auburn

A memorial plaque (Korea) is located by Bicentennial Park.

Berlin

A plaque in a rock lists the names of those who served in the Korean Conflict, and it has an engraving of a map of Korea, an airplane and a GI. It is located in Veterans Park.[81]

Concord

The Manchester Street Bridge is located here.[82]

Derry

A memorial (Korea and Vietnam) can be found in MacGregor Park on East Broadway.

Enfield

A Korean War monument is located on Route 4 near High Street in Veterans Memorial Park.

Franklin

A plaque on a rock is located at the end of Webster Bridge.

Groveton

A memorial (Korea) is located in the town square.

Hampstead

A granite slab with the outline of the country of Korea can be found on the town green.

Haverhill

A plaque can be found on the village green.

The Korean Conflict monument in Jacob Square, Hooksett. *Sheila Bailey.*

Hooksett

Hooksett's Korea monument is located in Jacob Square.

Hopkinton

Veterans Park is located across from the Congregational church on Route 103.

Jaffrey

Memorial Park is located on River Street.

Lyndeborough

A plaque mounted on granite is located on the grounds of J.A. Tarbell Library in Lyndeborough.

Manchester

Private First Class Roger B. Cote Square is located here.[83]

Nashua

Monuments honoring veterans of all major American wars, including Korea, were dedicated on July 1, 1989, at the Deschenes Oval in the middle of Railroad Square.

There is a memorial to Gilbert "Lefty" Dumais, the first Nashua man killed in the Korean War on August 19, 1950, in Atherton Park.

Newington

One of three stone monuments at Nimble Hill Road, south of the town library, honors those who served in the Korean War.

Northwood

A memorial can be found at the town hall complex.

Portsmouth

A trifold monument to the Vietnam Korean Wars and POW/MIAs was erected by the Sons of the American Legion in 2004.

Sutton

A plaque is set on Pillsbury Memorial Hall.

Wakefield

A monument to the veterans of the Korean, Vietnam and Persian Gulf Wars was donated by Lyman F. Holmes Post 2663 on June 21, 1998, and is located near town hall.

6

My Brother's Keeper?

The Vietnam War

The Vietnam War was a war that divided America, raising questions that have plagued us ever since, including the $64,000 one: When do we intervene?

The names and images have burned themselves into our collective memory—My Lai, Gulf of Tonkin Resolution, Tet Offensive, the fallout spreading to Laos and Cambodia, Kent State and a college student weeping over a friend who would never grow a day older, desperate people crowding onto rooftops in Saigon. It was the first televised war and the last to which we sent people who didn't want to go.

The war in Indochina started in 1946, when French troops occupied Vietnam after Japan's defeat in the Second World War. The French surrendered to the Viet Minh at Dien Bien Phu in May 1954. The Geneva Accords in July divided Vietnam at the seventeenth parallel into a North supported by China, Russia and other Communist countries, and a South supported by the United States, Australia and other democracies. The United States began advising in 1954 and gradually built up sixteen thousand troops by 1963. When a North Vietnamese torpedo boat attacked two American destroyers in the Gulf of Tonkin, President Lyndon B. Johnson submitted the Gulf of Tonkin Resolution to Congress, authorizing the executive branch to "take all necessary measures to repel any armed attack against the forces of the United States."

The rationale for the war was to keep South Vietnam from becoming communist, and the "domino theory" coined by President Dwight D.

Eisenhower became a rallying cry for Americans who supported the war. But the North Vietnamese proved to be powerful enemies.

Broadcasters, such as CBS's Walter Cronkite, brought the war into American living rooms. In 1968, Cronkite reported on the deaths of five hundred unarmed villagers in what became known as the My Lai massacre. Millions of people took to the streets in 1968 and 1969 to protest the country's involvement in Vietnam. By 1970, when members of the Ohio National Guard shot unarmed college students at Kent State University, approximately fifty thousand Americans had been killed in Vietnam. The swell of protest became a tidal wave.

Men of draft age flowed across the border into Canada, or they let themselves be drafted and then deserted. Between July 1966 and December 1973, more than five hundred thousand military personnel vanished.

The war was a catalyst for other social change, including recreational drug use, loosened sexual mores and the challenge to almost everything the Greatest Generation had worked to preserve. Fathers didn't recognize their sons or daughters. Racial tensions boiled over—or didn't—as the fluid Age of Aquarius absorbed people of all skin tones. By the time the last of the Americans and South Vietnamese had climbed onto those helicopters on April 29, 1975, the country would never be the same again.

And the dominoes had fallen. In 1976, Vietnam was unified as the Socialist Republic of Vietnam. Cambodia and Laos also remain Communist countries.

The United States spent more than $120 billion on a war it didn't win, resulting in oil shortages and widespread inflation. But its largest cost was in human capital. Millions of men and women suffered from PTSD, which would become a household term in the veteran community. Many, especially the men, would experience alcoholism, drug abuse, the splintering of their families and homelessness. The war also introduced America to the fallout from Agent Orange, a herbicide sprayed in Vietnam, Laos and Cambodia with the intent of depriving the enemy of food and vegetation for cover. Exposure to the herbicide has been linked to certain cancers and other health problems. And in a study done by the VA and Stanford University School of Medicine, Vietnam veterans were twice as likely to suffer from depression and anxiety than veterans of any other war.[84]

The country and the state were slow to pay tribute to the war in general. Initially, there was too much shame and too much blame. In November 1982, the national Vietnam Veterans Memorial opened in Washington, D.C. The design by Maya Lin features two slabs of polished black granite bearing the names of those who died. The two slabs are each 246 feet, 9 inches long, and at their apex, they are 10 feet tall. The starkness of the design provoked initial controversy and concern. To counter the negative reaction, the committee asked Frederick Hart, who had placed third in the original design competition, to create something more conventional. He responded with a bronze figural monument of *Three Soldiers*. But over the years, the wall has grown on Americans, both in its fixed position in Washington, D.C., and in several traveling iterations.

As with the memorials to the Korean War, the Vietnam War's memorials saw the final turning away from ornamental statuary and mythical figures. The truth was enough to grapple with.

Though the memorials were no longer flowery or figural, Jim Pope, a Vietnam veteran from Brookline, posited that there's a reason for that, and it has nothing to do with national shame. Pope thinks Korea and Vietnam pointed to the fact that "we don't have 'heroes' anymore. We've recognized that war is a group effort, and maybe that's the way it should be."

But New Hampshire continued to recognize what it saw as heroes—without fanfare but with a quiet appreciation.

This Vietnam marker can be found in the Veterans' Cemetery, Elm Street, Manchester. It shows the stark geometric style of a Vietnam monument, if they got one at all. *Sheila Bailey.*

Above: The Vietnam monument in Jacob Square, Hooksett. It reflects a starkness and bleakness, especially when compared with the World War II monument a few feet away. But then, what was there to say? *Sheila Bailey.*

Left: Jedh Barker. *Department of Defense.*

Opposite: The plaque on Franklin Town Hall honoring Jedh Barker. *Sheila Bailey.*

New Hampshire's small towns love hard and long, especially when the object of the affection is a member of the armed forces. Franklin, New Hampshire, never forgot Jedh Barker, even though he had moved from New Hampshire when he was six. Barker was born on June 20, 1945, in Franklin. He was a star athlete in high school in Paramus, New Jersey, and completed two years of college before enlisting in the Marines. He achieved the rank of lance corporal. In Vietnam, he was a participant in Operation Kingfisher. His platoon was attacked by North Vietnamese troops. The platoon got under cover. When a grenade was thrown, Barker jumped onto it, saving the lives of his fellow Marines. Barker died on September 21, 1967, at Leatherneck Square near Con Thien, Quan Tri Province.

Barker posthumously received the Medal of Honor. His heroism is noted by his hometown of Paramus, where he is buried, and he is also listed on the Vietnam War Monument.[85] And Franklin never forgot. A memorial plaque listing Barker's achievements and sacrifice is set on the front of city hall.

Though group memorials did not come for a while, towns honored their individual losses with dignity—and said their names. The town of Hooksett mourned Private First Class Arthur C. Mourtgis, its first Vietnam fatality. He is honored with a memorial at Jacob Square, the town's veterans park, and was buried in Manchester's Mount Calvary Cemetery.

Arthur Mourtgis was the first Hooksett man to die in Vietnam. He is memorialized in the town's Jacob Square. *Sheila Bailey*.

But the Vietnam War and the years following also marked the turn toward a different way to remember. Instead of a slab of granite or a sheet of copper, the memorials were often things the young men would have liked or used. (Exeter rechristened a swimming pool after fallen Navy SEAL Dan Healy.)[86] Their names began appearing on playing fields, community centers and recreational areas.

Marine corporal William G. Fraser died in Vietnam. His town of Hooksett named one of its parks for him, and it was dedicated on November 11, 1968. He was buried in the nearby Holy Rosary Cemetery. Patricia Bouchard of Hooksett remembers Fraser: he was her nephew, even though only two years separated them. "My half sister was thirty years older than me, and he was her son," Bouchard explained. She recalls Fraser was "a nice guy. He played the piano, not just simple things, but classical." He played at his own grammar school graduation and in recitals, according to Bouchard. Fraser was engaged at the time of his death, and according to Bouchard, the girl never married. "When his mother and father died, she came to their funeral," Bouchard said. "When we were cleaning out their house, I gave her some things of his."

Marine corporal William G. Fraser of Hooksett was killed in Vietnam. *Chase-Bouchard family.*

It was a sad day when Bouchard heard about her nephew's death, according to her. Her father was reading a newspaper and came upon an item about a Marine scout who got out of his helicopter and was killed. She remembers her father saying, "I bet that was Bill."

Friends and relatives turned out for the funeral, along with much of Hooksett. Bouchard was only eighteen at the time, and her sharpest memory is the Marine guard who accompanied the body and stayed throughout the entire funeral. "My sister and her husband were never the same," Bouchard recalled. "They were older, and he was their only child." At eighteen years old, Bouchard missed her nephew but wasn't really concerned with the war in general. "It was only when I got older and read about it that I thought, 'What the heck were they doing?'"

Fraser's mother kept a scrapbook, and when she died, it passed to Bouchard. Bouchard's daughter Amy Chase teaches school in another district, and when Chase accompanied the eighth graders to Washington, D.C., she helped them find her cousin's name on the Vietnam Veterans Memorial. She also uses the material to teach students about the conflict that affected their grandfathers, great-grandfathers and the nation.

The park was a good memorial to Fraser, Bouchard said. She remembers there was a corner store nearby owned by the Duplessix family, and the neighborhood kids spent their nickels there. "They had ponies, and they'd give kids a ride," she said. Though the days of corner stores are all but gone, the park remains. Bouchard's daughter took her baby to play there, and the senior Bouchards have stopped by a time or two. "It's so nice there," Bouchard said. "I think he would have liked it."

Manchester sent boys like Winston Taggart, a twenty-year-old killed in action in December 1967. His family was never certain if he'd been killed or was missing in action, despite the telegram. The Army sent a sealed casket, his clothing and a packet of letters from his mother. But there was no closure, and the Taggarts wondered for twenty-one years.

In 1988, Taggart's childhood friend Richard Gosselin visited the replica of the Vietnam Veterans Memorial as it traveled through Texas. Gosselin found Winston's name and began to reminisce to his wife. A stranger

Fraser's town of Hooksett named one of its athletic fields for the lifelong resident, and it was dedicated on November 11, 1968. *Sheila Bailey.*

standing next to him, Frank Mares of Houston, stared at the name. Mares was on the tank with Taggart on December 19, 1967, when it hit a mine. Mares told Gosselin he had been wondering how to contact Winston's family but only knew that they were in New Hampshire. Mares made the long drive to New Hampshire to tell the Taggarts about Taggart's last days.[87] It was a miracle at a time when miracles were desperately needed.

The Goffes Falls community raised money for a carillon to play hymns from Bethany Chapel. The bells did toll for Taggart, both literally and figuratively, and the tribute remains in his old neighborhood.

Manchester also sent men like Lucien Tessier, who died on February 19, 1968, in Hue, South Vietnam, while piloting a helicopter on a supply mission to the Marines fighting at Hue. He was a captain in the marine corps. The young pilot volunteered to fly a "mercy mission" to evacuate one dozen injured Marines at Hue. He was twenty-five at the time.[88]

Manchester also contributed five men from the West Side, buddies from the close French Canadian enclave who died on the same day. Though the men would never grow a day older, it was a coming of age for a shaken community. *Union Leader* reporter Shawne K. Wickham wrote in her fifty-year follow-up, "That summer, Americans were transfixed by televised images of the moon landing, and the younger generation celebrated rock and roll and free love at a music festival on a farm in upstate New York. But

Winston Taggart of Manchester died in the Vietnam War. He was from the Goffes Falls section of the city, and the carillon at the Goffes Falls Chapel, now Bethany Chapel, was dedicated in his memory. *Sheila Bailey.*

the news that rocked New Hampshire was the loss of these young men in a far-off jungle."[89]

Roger Robichaud, Richard Genest, Richard Raymond, Gaetan Beaudoin and Guy Blanchette were killed on August 26, 1969, when the truck they were riding in struck a landmine. They were scheduled to come home the following week, and they did come home—in flag-draped coffins. Two thousand people crowded into Manchester's small airport to welcome them home. The Right Reverend Ernest J. Primeau, the bishop of Manchester, met the fallen soldiers at what was then Grenier Field. Mayor John Mongan called it the "saddest day in Manchester's history."[90] The Sunday paper went on to report:

> *The family members huddled at the edge of the crowd as the first casket was wheeled across the runway on its silver-colored cart; the honor guard started its drum roll as the spectators became silent.*
>
> *But then the moans and sobs of relatives were heard above the silence: a small boy flung his arms up across his face and called "Daddy" as the second casket was wheeled toward the crowd, and young wives bent forward into the arms of their elders.[91]*

Maine resident Celine Therrien, formerly of Manchester, remembers that August: "I went to high school with Roger Robichaud," she said. "He was in my husband's class, three years ahead of me. I also knew his sister Sue." She remembered Robichaud, a 1964 graduate who was tall and handsome, "a nice guy." He wanted to go to school to be a funeral director, she recalled, and he had that kind of presence.

It was a different world back then, with the West Side a city within a city. Families still spoke French at home—and sometimes in the area's shops and businesses. In her parochial elementary school, Therrien learned for half of the day in French and half in English. The neighborhood had its own high school, Sainte Marie, but it was small. "My graduating class," she said, "had forty-five students."

Until they were in high school, West Side kids stayed pretty much close to home, Therrien recalled. When they were old enough to ride the bus alone, they went into mainstream Manchester for shopping, movies and dances at other schools. "We got discriminated against, they called us names sometimes, but we just took it," she said with a shrug. She was a young wife with an infant in August 1969, living in the Pinardville section of Goffstown when she heard about the deaths. "I read about it in the paper, and my first thought was, 'They were on their way home.'"

The rebuilt Amoskeag Bridge in Manchester was dedicated to Manchester's men who were lost in Vietnam, including five National Guardsmen who were killed on the same day. *Sheila Bailey*.

The plaque naming the Amoskeag Bridge for Manchester residents killed in Vietnam, including five National Guardsmen who lost their lives on the same day. *Sheila Bailey*.

The news rocked the close-knit community, Therrien recalled. "It was a terrible time for the West Side. We were all grieving." Robichaud left a wife, and Therrien recalled, "I felt sorry for his poor widow. So young." Raymond was twenty-seven; Robichaud, twenty-four; Genest, twenty-four; Blanchette, twenty-two; and Beaudoin, twenty. Most of all, Therrien recalled, the deaths of the Five Guardsmen brought in the outside world. "It was not a world we wanted to let in," she said.

The city memorialized the Five Guardsmen and its other Vietnam heroes by dedicating the rebuilt Amoskeag Bridge in their honor. In addition, there are memorials at the National Guard headquarters in Concord and at the Guard building in Manchester.

Vietnam was divisive—but not in Manchester, a city that took care of its own.

LISTINGS: THE VIETNAM WAR

Acworth

A tribute is located in Memorial Park.

Alstead

A plaque on a rock in the town center was dedicated in 2008 and was donated by Alstead's veterans.

Alton

An asymmetrical piece of granite holds the names of Alton men who served, and relief images of three weary soldiers and can be seen on Main Street (Route 11) when traveling north.

Antrim

Memorial Park is located on Jameson Avenue.

Atkinson

A memorial is located near town hall.

Auburn

A memorial plaque (Vietnam) can be found in Bicentennial Park.

Berlin

A plaque in a rock is located in Veterans Park on Glen Avenue.

POW/MIA *Bracelet* was erected by the White Mountains Veterans Council on September 16, 2005, in Veterans Park.

Boscawen

The Martin L. Gillespie Memorial, Navy Cross (Vietnam) is located in State Veterans Cemetery.

The New Hampshire State Vietnam War Memorial lists the 227 men of New Hampshire who lost their lives in the war. It can be found in the Grove of Memorials at the New Hampshire State Veterans Cemetery on U.S. Route 3, north of Boscawen.

Charlestown

A monument to those who gave their lives in defense of freedom and democracy in Vietnam, Lebanon, Grenada, Panama and the Persian Gulf Wars can be found at the intersection of Main Street (Route 12) and Depot Road, on the left when traveling north on Main Street. It includes David E. Gardner, who died in Vietnam, and Todd C. Rich, who died in the Persian Gulf.

Chester

A memorial is located at the intersection of Chester Street and Derry Road.

Chesterfield

A small monument in Ware's Grove, Spofford, displays two names, Specialist 4 William Wayne O'Neil, Army, and First Lieutenant Howard Kaiser, Air Force.

Dunbarton

A memorial (Vietnam) is set on a granite plaque on a boulder at town hall.

Enfield

An honor roll is located in Veterans Memorial Park.

Franklin

The Jedh Barker Memorial is located here. He received the Congressional Medal of Honor (Vietnam) after dying on September 21, 1967. The memorial was dedicated in 1990 at the town hall.[92]

Hampstead

A granite slab with an outline of the country of Vietnam and a helicopter is located on the town green.

Hampton

A monument (Vietnam) is set in a plaque in rock at the courthouse.

Hill

The Chester L. Butcher, U.S. Navy, memorial bench can be found in Veterans Park.

Hooksett

A memorial was erected in Jacob Square to Private First Class Arthur C. Mourtgis Jr., who died in 1967. He was the first Hooksett serviceperson to give his life in the Vietnam War. He was a member of the 3rd Battalion, 7th

Infantry, 199th Infantry Brigade. Mourtgis posthumously received the Purple Heart and was buried in Manchester's Mount Calvary Cemetery.[93]

Fraser Field was dedicated on November 11, 1968. The Town of Hooksett dedicated this playing field to the memory of Marine corporal William G. Fraser. Fraser was a lifetime resident of Hooksett and was a Hooksett serviceman who died in Vietnam. He died on December 28, 1967.[94]

Manchester

A monument is located in Veterans Park.

The renamed Amoskeag Bridge's plaque is located at the National Guard Armory.[95]

The Winston Taggart Memorial Carillon is located in the Goffes Falls neighborhood.[96]

Nashua

The Vietnam War Memorial was one of the several monuments erected in the Deschenes Oval in Nashua's Railroad Square.

The names of eighteen Nashua-area men who died in Vietnam are listed at Vietnam Memorial Park at Ledge Street School.

Newington

A stone monument is engraved with an honor roll for those who served in Vietnam, Lebanon, Grenada and Panama War. There is a stone monument with an honor roll on Nimble Hill Road for those who served in the Gulf War and the War on Terror.

New Boston

A scenic drive, a three-and-a-half-mile stretch, is a designated area honoring Sergeant Ronald Charles Davis, Fourth Infantry Division, who died on January 23, 1970, in Binh Dinh, Vietnam.

New Ipswich

The Veterans Memorial was dedicated in 2000 on the town green.

North Woodstock/Woodstock

A plaque is mounted on a granite monument, honoring those who served in Vietnam. It was dedicated on November 1, 1983, in Soldiers Park in North Woodstock.

A plaque honoring POW/MIAs is located on Lost River Road.

Webster

William R. Pearson Memorial Park was dedicated to Pearson, who was killed in Vietnam on April 6, 1972. It is located on Route 127 behind Webster Elementary School.

A New Reality

Iraq and Afghanistan

Vietnam was the last war to which we sent children. The draft ended in 1973. The post-Vietnam era has been marked by conflict in Iraq (twice), Afghanistan and other fields. But the men and then women who fought them knew what they were getting into and knew why they were doing it. They were motivated young people, some with degrees, who served their country because they wanted to. Atkinson's Jeremy Graczyk was the valedictorian of his high school class. Plymouth's Doug DiCenzo graduated from West Point.

Many of the enlistees grew up in the shadow of 9/11 and saw the events of that tragic day unfold. Others were spurred to serve their country in the First and Second Gulf Wars or Afghanistan.

The first Gulf War originated in August 1990, after Iraq, under dictator Saddam Hussein, invaded and occupied Kuwait. The move brought immediate censure from the international community, sanctions by the United Nations and forces deployed by the United States and United Kingdom. Eventually, a thirty-nine-country coalition was formed under U.S. general Norman Schwarzkopf Jr.

Kuwait was liberated in February 1991, with most Iraqi troops surrendering. But in his own country, Hussein went on dictating.

President George H.W. Bush's administration received criticism for allowing Saddam's regime to remain in power. The issue was to be revisited in 2001, after the September 11 attacks on the Pentagon and World Trade Center. The Second Iraq War began in March 2003 with the "shock and awe" bombing of Baghdad.

Though President George W. Bush said the initiative was to uncover "weapons of mass destruction" stockpiled by Saddam's regime, no significant stores were ever found. But the coalition forces didn't go away empty-handed. Saddam Hussein was captured in December of that year, under an initiative called "Operation Red Dawn." He was executed on December 30, 2006.

The United States withdrew its troops from Iraq in 2011.

The War in Afghanistan has the dubious distinction of being America's longest-running war, surpassing Vietnam and lasting from 2001 to 2021. Following the September 11, 2001 attacks, President George W. Bush demanded that the Taliban, a religious and paramilitary organization that was running the country, extradite Osama Bin Laden, the mind behind the terrorist attacks. The Taliban refused, and the War in Afghanistan was launched. It ran five months longer than the Vietnam War. Though Bin Laden was rooted out, the Taliban regained power after the United States left in August 2021.

Military personnel then included women, and both men and women faced struggles when they survived and came home. While they weren't castigated like the Vietnam troops, neither Gulf War nor Afghanistan veterans enjoyed the overwhelming support that the veterans of World War II received. No one planted victory gardens. No one kissed nurses in Times Square. And younger veterans didn't always want to join the VFW or the American Legion. Many suffered their post-traumatic stress disorders alone.

Veterans of the first Gulf War also suffered physically from a condition known as Gulf War syndrome. The illness is characterized by chronic fatigue, fibromyalgia and gastrointestinal disorders, and the causes of the illness remain undetermined. A higher number of birth defects, including heart valve and kidney issues, continue to be found in these veterans' children.

But New Hampshire supported its veterans. In every small town, signs welcomed the heroes home, from the library to the town hall and churches. Old sheets and spray paint became homemade signs hung from overpasses. Organizations, such as the Pease Greeters, a group of civilians welcoming troops home to Pease Air National Guard Base, made sure the troops knew they were appreciated. And new monuments went up.

Plymouth's Doug DiCenzo was a husband, a father and a hero to his wife and boy. Ultimately, he became a hero to many more.

Douglas DiCenzo was a standout athlete at Plymouth High School, serving as the captain of the football and wrestling teams. He was the class president and a member of the National Honor Society, and when he was accepted at the U.S. Military Academy at West Point, his home city expected

Army captain Douglas DiCenzo, a native of Plymouth, lost his life to a roadside bomb in Iraq in 2006. *Nicole DiCenzo.*

even more good things from him. He completed the Army's airborne and ranger courses and met his wife, Nicole, while he was stationed in Columbus, Georgia. They lived on a post in Fairbanks, Alaska, returned to Columbus and then were stationed in Germany. He was a company commander for C Company in the First Armored Division, Second Brigade, based in Baumholder, Germany. DiCenzo's son, Dakin, was born in 2003.

DiCenzo was eventually deployed to Iraq, where a roadside bomb took his life on May 23, 2006. His widow, Nicole, remembers that day. She had known military life would mean a lot of traveling, frequent moves and sometimes being left alone. She was twenty-nine when they were married, and she and Doug knew she was independent enough to handle that. But the other reality of military life, the war zone, struck her after September 11, 2001. "Doug came home and said, 'We're going to be deployed.'" While the brass eventually sent another unit instead, "that was the first time it hit home," DiCenzo recalled. "At some point, I knew he was going to be gone."

Doug was deployed to Iraq. Nicole and her son stayed behind at the base in Germany with other Army wives in an atmosphere she described as "a college dorm." "We were always in and out of each other's apartments." She and a friend were watching *America's Got Talent* when she heard the knock on the door. When she saw the Army personnel standing outside, she knew. "Your whole body goes into shock when they say the word," DiCenzo recalled. "Your world stops. It's like an out-of-body experience." The whole complex soon knew, and six Army wives eventually joined her for a vigil that would become familiar to many of them.

There was nothing for Nicole in Germany, and she moved to New Hampshire. "The day I got on the plane, I had nothing but my kid and a couple of bags." She had lost two pets and Doug while in Germany, and her world was compressed to her son and those two suitcases.

DiCenzo had the use of Doug's grandmother's house, and she and Dakin settled in. She found healing in Plymouth. In true New England fashion, the three-thousand-member community "knew who I was and left me alone."

Nicole DiCenzo shows the memorial dedicated to her husband, Captain Doug DiCenzo, to their toddler son. Dakin is a teenager now, and his mother works to keep Doug's memory—and sacrifice—alive. *Nicole DiCenzo.*

She eventually relocated to Georgia to be near her own family and some Army friends; there, she raised her son and started a Bible-teaching ministry.

Doug DiCenzo is remembered by his home state with a monument on the west end of the bridge over the Pemigewasset River and a camp fund to help children enjoy the outdoors. A memorial golf tournament run by his relatives raises money for the camp fund. His bridge was dedicated on May 26, 2008.

Nicole DiCenzo notes that the current trend is to keep the loved one's memory alive rather than bury it, and she's all for that. "The way they do things now—it's wonderful." She raised her son, "Dak," by taking him to celebrations of life for Doug and other lost servicemen and an annual September 11 memorial, and she enrolled him with a volunteer group that takes military kids hunting. "Some of the men knew Doug, so they can talk with him," she said.

Nicole is pleased with the efforts to honor Doug, such as her in-laws' golf tournament to fund camp scholarships, but she's even more pleased with an initiative close to home. "My mother-in-law, Cathy Crane, had people who knew Doug write letters about him. I've saved them for my son, and occasionally, he'll read a couple." She concluded, "It's important for Dak to know the impact of what his dad did."

Atkinson's Jeremy Graczyk could have been anything. He was the valedictorian of his class at Timberlane Regional High School, qualified for the United States Naval Academy and was a two-time college All-American standout in rugby. He joined the United States Marine Corps, rising to the rank of major in 2009.

Graczyk led Marines in the initial invasion of Iraq in Operation Iraqi Freedom in 2003. He later served as a platoon commander of a force renaissance unit and as an infantry company commander in Iraq. He was deployed seven times to Afghanistan and Africa. He earned three Navy–Marine Corps Commendation Medals, one Navy–Marine Corps Achievement Medal, two Combat Action Ribbons, two National Defense Service Medals, two Afghanistan Campaign Medals, five Iraq Campaign Medals, the Global War on Terrorism Service Medal, the Presidential Unit Citation, a Meritorious Unit Citation and seven Sea Service Deployment Ribbons. He also received a posthumous Bronze Star and Bronze Star with Valor.

Ever the outdoorsman, Graczyk died on Tuesday, July 12, 2011, in a BASE jumping accident in Switzerland. He is remembered with a monument and a nonprofit, the JG Live Free or Die Memorial Fund, whose main fundraiser is an annual 5K race. He is listed on the Timberlane High School Hero's Wall.

In 1996, Airman First Class Peter Morgera of Stratham died in a terrorist bombing at the Khobar Towers in Saudi Arabia. He was one of nineteen U.S. Air Force airmen killed when a truck bomb exploded outside Khobar Towers on the night of June 25, 1996. He was a member of the Stratham Volunteer Fire Department, and a room at the fire station is named after him.

Andrew Stevens, also from Stratham, always knew he'd be in some branch of the military. His father, John, was a petty officer in the Coast Guard reserve, his brother John is an Air Force pilot and his sister Rachel Stevens Metz is a senior airman in the Air Force. Stevens, a graduate of Exeter High School, lost his life in the crash of a Black Hawk helicopter at Fort Drum, New York, in March 2003. The UH-60L Black Hawk had just completed a routine assault exercise and was on its way back to an airfield when it crashed in a remote part of the rugged, 167-square-mile post in northern New York. The crash took the life of Private First Class Stevens (twenty) and ten other soldiers. Stevens's unit, the Tenth Mountain Division Polar Bears, was scheduled to ship out to Iraq at the time of his death. The War with Iraq began eight days later. He is memorialized by his hometown with a granite bench in Stratham Hill Park.

Floyd Burlock, the commander of the Berlin VFW Post, doesn't cry easily. But the Vietnam veteran tears up when he talks about Randy Rosenberg. "I knew him really well," Burlock recalled. "He worked for me at Berlin City Ford." And Burlock "talked him into joining the military." Burlock, a veteran with twenty-eight years of service in the U.S. Air Force, knew the service is a good career for some. "When people don't know what to do after high school, I always recommend the military," he said. He did the same for Rosenberg when the younger man was pondering his future. He thought the Army would be a good fit for Rosenberg, and he was right. "He was an outstanding employee—did above and beyond," Burlock recalled, and that work ethic translated to the service. "He was promoted ahead of his peers."

The Army sergeant died on January 24, 2004, when an explosive device detonated in the vehicle he was riding in. The Berlin native was stationed in Khalidiya, Iraq. Burlock was at work when he heard about Rosenberg's death, and it really hit him, he said, in a different way from other deaths or even the deaths of his own colleagues who had died in Thailand. "He was a hometown boy, and it just struck home," Burlock said.

Left: Berlin named a stretch of road after army sergeant Randy Rosenberg, a hometown boy who lost his life in Iraq. *Floyd Burlock.*

Right: Army sergeant Randy Rosenberg of Berlin died on January 24, 2004, in Iraq when an explosive device detonated in the vehicle he was riding in. *Floyd Burlock.*

Burlock wishes Rosenberg could have come back to Berlin, and he's pleased with the way the town and general population treat returning Iraq and Afghanistan veterans. Korean veterans didn't get much recognition—and Vietnam even less, he mused. But Berlin did right by Rosenberg, Burlock added. "We dedicated a road to him," he said. "I thought that was fantastic." Rosenberg is also honored in the recently remodeled Veterans Park, he said.

Navy SEAL Daniel Healy was killed in 2005; he was the first graduate of Exeter High School to die during the War on Terror. Chief Petty Officer Healy, a native of the town, died in Afghanistan on June 28, 2005. After four of his men were reported lost, Healy boarded a rescue helicopter, though his rank would have allowed him to stay behind. He took some of the rescue crew off the lead helicopter and boarded it himself, saying famously, "Those are my men, and my face will be the first one they see." Of the original four men on the mission, three were killed by Taliban troops. One, Marcus Luttrell, survived and is the subject of the book *Lone Survivor* and the 2013 film of the same name.

The Town of Exeter renamed its community swimming pool in Healy's honor, and a monument to Healy and the Redwing crew is also on the property. He also has a foundation made in his name that is funded by an annual 5K run.

Healy's mother, Natalie, has since made a career of fighting for veterans and Gold and Blue Star families and memorializing the lost. But when she learned of Dan's death in June 2005, she didn't automatically make the connection to a memorial. "To be honest, I didn't know they were doing things like that," she said. She was busy with the press, funeral arrangements and running her own business. "I felt like I did my grieving part time," Healy admitted. And in the brave new world of post-Vietnam conflict, she wasn't aware that monuments were still being constructed.

In 2008, the idea for a permanent memorial took shape. Healy's brother Patrick Carberry had a sculptor friend, Steve Green, and Green told the family he wanted to donate a monument. "I was thrilled, happy,' Healy recalled. "By then, I knew we were doing things like that." Healy approved of the design but insisted on two things. One, she wanted all the names of Dan's unit up there. "The SEALs are such a tight-knit group," she said. And she wanted John 15:13 on the monument somewhere. John 15:13 states that "greater love hath no man than that he lay down his life for his brother." "That's the SEALs," Healy said. "They're all brothers."

Healy never asked the town of Exeter for a memorial, and she was completely surprised to learn that the town had renamed the pool in Dan's

Left: The community swimming pool in Exeter New Hampshire was renamed for Navy Seal Chief Petty Officer Daniel Healy, a native of the town, who died in Afghanistan on June 28, 2005. He also has a foundation in his name, funded by an annual 5K run. This monument to Healy and the Operation Redwing crew stands near the pool area. *Sheila Bailey.*

Below: Dan Healy, an officer, didn't have to go with the team to rescue four Navy SEALs lost in the mountains of Afghanistan. He went anyway, because he wanted "my face to be the first one they see." *Sheila Bailey.*

GREATER LOVE HATH NO MAN THAN HE LAY DOWN HIS LIFE FOR HIS BROTHERS JOHN 15:13

honor. The formal dedication of the pool took place on the same day as the formal dedication of the statue. The town also named the bridge over Guinea Road in honor of Dan, she said. And she and a friend started the 5K race soon after.

The original monument included a picture of Dan painted on porcelain, Healy recalled. The porcelain image was broken, replaced and broken again. Healy's daughter put out a Facebook appeal, and donors from all over the country sent money to fix it. The final installation was an unbreakable portrait on metal, she said.

But there was donation money left over, and Healy didn't feel comfortable keeping it. She wanted to establish a foundation to provide assistance to veterans, single-parent families and students in need of scholarships. She and a friend decided to augment the funds with a road race, "about which I knew nothing," Healy said with a laugh. But her friend knew about races, and Healy has a marketing background, so they went for it. The race has done well, with an average of 250 entrants and $30,000 raised each year, and it's one more way to keep Dan's memory alive, she said. "He would be happy," she said, "that we're using his name to raise money to help people."

Healy approves of the way today's war casualties are honored. "It's wonderful," she said, adding, "It makes up for the way we treated the Vietnam veterans." And she's in favor of anything that humanizes the troops, both those lost and those who come home. "People have to remember, it's not just faceless people in some distant place making the world safe from terrorists. It's our friends, our neighbors who are making the sacrifices." And their mothers.

When the monument was being set up in 2009 at the Exeter Recreation Complex, Healy went over in the morning to watch prior to the afternoon dedication. A woman was sitting at a picnic table with two small boys. Healy remembers one of the boys coming over to her, "with his eyes as big as saucers. He said, 'A soldier died.'"

"And I said, 'Yes, that's my little boy,'" Healy said.

LISTINGS: POST-VIETNAM CONFLICTS AND WARS, ALL WARS POW/MIA

Acworth

A tribute can be found in Memorial Park.

Albany

A memorial to all wars can be found at town hall on Route 13.

Andover

A memorial to all wars between the Revolution and World War I can be found on the town green.

Atkinson

The Jeremy Graczyk Memorial is located on the town common.[97]

Bartlett

A memorial to all wars is located at the intersection of Main Street and Albany Avenue and can be seen on the left when traveling west on Main Street.

Barrington

A monument to all wars can be found in Pine Grove Cemetery on Route 9.

Bedford

A monument to all wars can be found in Bedford Village Common.

Barrington honors all its residents who served with this monument in the Pine Grove Cemetery. *Sheila Bailey.*

Berlin

Gulf War casualty Randy Rosenberg is remembered by his hometown of Berlin with a monument and a renamed road.[98]

Veterans Memorial Bridge on Twelfth Street is dedicated to all veterans.

Canaan

A plaque honoring those who served in Panama, Kuwait, Bosnia, the two Gulf Wars and Afghanistan can be found in town center.

Canterbury

A monument to all wars can be found in the town center.

Carroll

A monument to all wars is located on the town green.

Colebrook/Stewartstown

A monument to those who served in Lebanon, Panama and the Gulf War can be found on the town green.

Concord

Veterans Park is located on the corner of Loudon and Pembroke Roads.

Derry

The Michael Geary Memorial Bridge is located on Route 102. Geary died in combat on December 8, 2010, while serving in Afghanistan with the Fox Company 2/9 U.S. Marine Corps.

Exeter

A monument and community pool dedicated to Chief Petty Officer Dan Healy are located on Hampton Road.[99]

Franconia/Lincoln

A memorial to Army Specialist David J. Stelmat (Iraq/Afghanistan) is located in Franconia Notch State Park. Stelmat grew up in Littleton and worked at Cannon Mountain. He wanted to be a medic and joined the Army after high school, was assigned to front-line duty instead and went to Afghanistan. After his discharge, he attended the New Hampshire Technical Institute with the intent of becoming an EMT. He joined the New Hampshire National Guard and was deployed to Helmand Province, Afghanistan, where he died in a roadside bombing at the age of twenty-two.

Franklin

A monument to all wars and the "supreme sacrifice" is located at 316 Central Street.

Freedom

A monument to all wars is located in front of the bandstand on Main Street.

Henniker

The Army Sergeant Russell M. Durgin Bridge is located on Route 114. Durgin died in action on June 13, 2006, in Afghanistan.

The Sean M. Powers Memorial Bridge, located on Route 127, is dedicated to the Marine veteran of two tours in Iraq who died in a motor vehicle accident while driving home from work as a Hopkinton police officer on August 14, 2008.

Hillsboro

A monument to all wars is located at 29 School Street. There is also a Memorial Day plaque.

There is a bench honoring those who served in Operation Iraqi Freedom.

Keene

A memorial to POW/MIA is included as part of Cheshire County's veterans memorial at 10 Central Square.

Littleton

The Veterans Memorial Bridge on Cottage Street is dedicated to those who served in all wars.

Mason

A monument to all wars can be found in the town common.

Merrimack

Veterans Memorial Park is located on Camp Sargent Road.

Nashua

New Hampshire's Purple Heart Trail runs from I-95 in Seabrook to Portsmouth, west on Route 4, then across the state from Durham to Lebanon and also along Route 3 from Massachusetts to the Canadian border. The Purple Heart Trail creates a symbolic system of roads, bridges and other monuments honoring those men and women who have been awarded the Purple Heart. For more information, visit www.purpleheart.org. A monument to Purple Heart recipients stands in the Deschenes Oval in Railroad Square.

This monument in Nashua's Deschenes Oval celebrates those honored with the Purple Heart. *Sheila Bailey.*

Newbury

A monument to all wars can be found on Route 103.

Newmarket

Newmarket Veterans Bridge over Lamprey River was dedicated on May 16, 2009.

New London

A monument to all wars can be found in the town common.

Northfield

A monument to all wars can be found at the intersection of Sargent and Park Streets.

The *Live Free or Die* monument is located at the intersection Park Street and Dearborn Road and can be seen on the right when traveling north on Park Street.

Plymouth

Plymouth has a monument to Doug DiCenzo, who gave his life in Iraq at the age of thirty.[100]

A monument to all wars is located in town hall.

Portsmouth

A monument to all wars is located in Goodwin Park.

There is also a monument to POW/MIA in Goodwin Park.

Town of Rindge

A granite block honoring all wars is located in Town Park.

Salisbury

The Veterans Monument is located at Salisbury Town Hall by the flagpole and Academy Hall at 9 Old Coach Road.

Stark

A black granite monument to all wars can be found in Town Park and was dedicated in 1995.

Stratham

Memorials to Andrew Stevens and Peter Morgera can be found in Stratham Hill Park.[101]

Wakefield

A granite monument to the Persian Gulf and the Global War on Terrorism can be found near town hall.

Webster

The Sergeant William J. Tracy Memorial Bridge on Route 127 was dedicated to Army sergeant William Tracy, who died while on duty on February 25, 2003, in a helicopter crash in Kuwait during Operation Enduring Freedom.

A Place to Reflect

The Cathedral of the Pines

Y ou notice the silence first. Though cars roar by on the two-lane road below, the highway feeding into it and the state road feeding into the highway, the Cathedral of the Pines is silent except for the hum of bees, the chirping of birds and the peal of bells marking the hour from a majestic carillon. The visitors on a summer day murmur and even whisper as they enjoy the flowers or read inscriptions on the stones. Even children are quiet here, though they may not yet know what "war" means.

It is a place that changes little with the years. The infamous ice storm of 2008 knocked down a number of the signature pines, leaving open vistas, but they're being restored. The physical structure never changes, just like the sober young man whose portrait hangs over the fireplace in Hilltop House, the welcome center. He is a man who will never age.

It is a place that grew out of one family's grief to touch other grieving families—and then the world.

It started with a dream, but it was not the dream that made it a reality. Sanderson "Sandy" Sloane and his young wife had picked out a hilltop spot in Rindge for their forever home. His parents, Sibyl and Douglas Sloane, had purchased the 128 acres for their four children, Douglas Jr., Sandy, Margaret and John "Jack," to build their homes. The property was completely wooded, but in 1938, a hurricane had ripped through and destroyed many of the signature pine trees, especially those on the 5-acre parcel Sandy had claimed for his own. But the loss created a panoramic view of Grand Monadnock Mountain and other mountain ranges.

When the United States entered what would become the Second World War, both Jack and Sandy enlisted in the Army Air Corps. Jack flew a B-26 bomber and survived many missions. Sandy flew a B-17. His plane was shot down over Germany in 1944, and the young airman did not survive.

His grieving family planned a memorial service for August 1945 on the land where he had planned to build his home. Family, friends and community members attended, and the seed for the Cathedral of the Pines took root.

Altar of the Nations

The first man-made structure, the Altar of the Nations, was built in 1946. The altar is made up of stones from all fifty states, and others represent the homes of all United States presidents from Harry Truman to Barack Obama (Hawaii). The stones represent Plymouth, Massachusetts, and Plymouth, England. Stones are incorporated from Lexington and Concord, Massachusetts, where the Revolution began, and Yorktown, where it ended. There are stones from the Parthenon in Athens and the Colosseum in Rome.

The Altar of the Nations includes stones from every U.S. state and several foreign countries. *Sheila Bailey.*

The stones came from Omaha Beach in Normandy, France, the site of the D-Day invasion (contributed by President Dwight D. Eisenhower). They came from the Pacific theater in Japan, the Coral Sea and the sands of Iwo Jima. The stones came from Korea, Vietnam and Iraq. President George W. Bush donated a stone from the Pentagon that survived the attack of September 11, 2001.

But the symbolism doesn't end there. The top of the altar is made of Maryland green marble that was taken from a quarry that straddles the Mason-Dixon line. The slabs on the right and left represent the North and South, and the central slab represents the restoration of the Union.

And the mortar for the altar is mixed with soil from Mount Zion in Jerusalem.

A stone from Koblenz, Germany, represents the spot where Sandy Sloane's plane was shot down in 1944. The mayor of Koblenz personally delivered the stone in 1969.

Women's Memorial Bell Tower

Bells ring from a carillon at specified intervals. It's nothing new or splashy, just the comforting hymns that the dead might have known in their lifetimes. Like the altar, the Women's Memorial Bell Tower is rich with symbolism. One side features an early pioneer woman, musket at the ready, willing to defend her home. Another wall's plaque represents the women of the armed forces, including those who served in the Army, Navy, Air Force, Marines and Coast Guard. The third shows Clara Barton, the founder of the American Red Cross, assisting a wounded Civil War soldier, and is meant to represent all the women who serve their country by nursing the troops. The fourth wall's plaque pays tribute to other women, including the Sisters of Charity, who nursed fallen troops; the Salvation Army and YMCA; women who served on the home front on farms and in shops so men could defend liberty; female war correspondents; and the indelible image of Rosie the Riveter.

Symbolism continues in the center fountain, which commemorates the lives of nurses lost to war. Twelve kinds of fruit hang from the tree: breadfruit, pear, fig, peach, olive, orange, avocado, apple, lemon, cherry, pomegranate, and plum. The tree symbolizes the "Tree of Life" in Revelation 22:1–2, "On each side of the river stood the tree of life, bearing twelve crops of fruit, yielding its fruit every month. And the leaves of the tree are for the healing of nations."

The Women's Memorial Bell Tower, completed in 1967, honors the women who served in the nation's conflicts. *Sheila Bailey*.

It's a symbolism not lost on visitors as they makes make their way to Hilltop House, the welcome center. A table offers free literature about the cathedral, and a small bookshelf offers a library to be perused on-site. There's a small lecture hall that can double as a chapel with deep chairs around a fieldstone fireplace. A likeness of Sandy Sloane, frozen forever in youth, hangs above the fireplace.

There are more rocks here, including one from Auschwitz in Poland. And with the stones from Koblenz and the Pacific theater, it makes its own silent plea: "Never again."

The site is for all faiths, with a carving of the *Shema* on two rocks leading to the chapel area.

Other spots, like a tucked-away grotto, inspire contemplation and worship.

The site is available and popular for weddings, and its Easter sunrise service draws worshippers from all around the country. But it's perhaps best seen on a sunny afternoon, when the breeze wafts over the hilltop and the flowers are a riot of color.

Lieutenant Sanderson Sloane was shot down over Germany in 1944. His loss inspired his parents to create the Cathedral of the Pines in Rindge, an outdoor memorial garden and worship center. A portrait of Sandy Sloane hangs above the fireplace in Hilltop House, the original lodge at the cathedral. *Sheila Bailey.*

Above: *The Shema*, carved on rock at the Cathedral of the Pines, serves to remind visitors that the cathedral is open to all faiths. *Sheila Bailey*.

Left: A grotto with a statue of the Virgin Mary inspires devotion and reflection. *Sheila Bailey*.

Gretchen Ziegler has seen the cathedral in every iteration for most of her life. Douglas Sloane was Ziegler's father's Scout leader back in Newton, Massachusetts, in the twentieth century. The troop was struggling, with just seven or eight boys, but it grew after "Mr. Sloane" took over. Her family grew close to the Sloanes, and she says, "He was like my third grandfather."

Both Douglas and Sibyl came from money, according to Ziegler, and they were generous with what they had. "He was like Santa Claus," she said of the elder Sloane. After Memorial Day and Fourth of July parades, Douglas Sloane would wave all the Boy Scouts into a local ice cream shop and treat them, 125 strong. But his ultimate act of generosity came with the cathedral.

Ziegler's family remained close to the Sloanes, and when Sandy died and they put the cathedral together, her dad was one of the first trustees. She followed him, having a forty-year relationship with the complex. "I've been a trustee on and off for forty years, chaired the board, filled in when we were between executive directors," she said. She currently cochairs the board with Bernard Hamprey. She interprets the cathedral for the dozens of bus tours that stop by in the fall, and she loves sharing the history and meaning of each space. The bell tower is relatively new, built in 1967, she says. The stone Hilltop House was expanded in 1981, and the museum moved to the basement and expanded. They still have items they can't put out, but the expansion was a good idea, according to Ziegler. "People come away saying, 'I've got to bring my dad here.' 'I've got to bring my mom.'"

During the coronavirus pandemic of 2020 and 2021, the buildings were closed during its height, but people came every day to walk the grounds, according to Ziegler.

The cathedral is free and open to the public, so there's no way of tracking guests. But Ziegler estimates that between forty thousand and fifty thousand people come through the gates each year. What draws them? "It's the feeling of peace," Ziegler believes. "With so few people going to church, the synagogue or their mosque these days, they need an outlet for their spirituality." And on a spring day when the trees are budding or a fall day when blazing trees draw the eye up to Mount Monadnock, that's as good a reason as any.

Appendix

The Merci Boxcar, the Marine Memorial, the Submarine Memorials at the Albacore, the Veterans Cemetery, the Wright Museum, the War Dog Memorial, Manchester's Squares and the Sculptors

New Hampshire and the greater community didn't only say "thank you" with chisels and stone. The Granite State abounds with other memorials and mementos of those who gave all—or were willing to.

HOW THE FRENCH SAID "THANKS": THE MERCI BOXCAR

Tony Travia remembers how it was. "We used to march from Post 43, the Jutras Post, to here on the last Sunday in September," he says. "We wore our uniforms. We honored the police officer of the year; we sometimes had the French ambassador from Boston."

"We" included the members of the Forty and Eight, formerly a subsidiary group of the American Legion and now operating on its own. The Forty and Eight, divided into groups called voitures, exists solely to support an aging treasure, the Merci Boxcar, which is currently located on Manchester's West Side.

The Merci Boxcar, a gift from the grateful French people, can be seen by appointment in its location on Manchester's West Side. *Sheila Bailey.*

The boxcar is one of forty-nine boxcars that were given by the country of France in grateful recognition of America's help in World War II. In addition to helping the Allies win the war, the United States funneled $40 million worth of food and supplies to war-torn France and Italy. The boxcars all arrived in New York Harbor on February 3, 1949, aboard the *Magellan.* They were stuffed with gifts and memorabilia. The New Hampshire boxcar landed first in Concord and then moved to Manchester in 1953.

"The idea came from World War I and World War II vets who wanted to do something for the American people," Travia says, adding, "The people of France filled these boxcars with gifts."

Travia carefully unlocks the brick building that houses the boxcar. The land was given by a priest, Monsignor Gilbert, and it will belong to the Forty and Eight as long as it holds the annual march. The march hasn't been held for a couple of years due first to apathy and then to COVID-19. But the Boxcar remains on Manchester's West Side, a symbol of gratitude for the Greatest Generation—and the generation before them. Travia notes that the boxcars used for the gifts originally carried soldiers to the front in World

War I. The boxcars were also used by Germans in the Second World War to carry POWs to Germany and Jews to concentration camps, Travia adds.

The original contents of the boxcar included gifts from every region of France. Some of these were passed on to New Hampshire residents and are now long gone, while others are being scanned in by Travia, who worries about damage and deterioration. Other presents from the French are in safekeeping at the St. Anselm College Museum. The boxcar also contains war memorabilia, including framed newspaper clippings, medals, awards and old black-and-white photos. Two of the smock-like Forty and Eight uniforms hang from pegs, and Travia hopes they will one day be worn again.

Though the boxcar came into New Hampshire with fanfare and press, awareness has since fallen off, according to Travia. He was a longtime American Legion member and didn't know about it until he was approached to join the Forty and Eight. "You can't just volunteer, you have to be recruited," he explains.

The Forty and Eight designation refers to what the boxcar should be able to carry—forty men or eight horses, according to Travia.

Tony Travia, a member of the Forty and Eight, shows off the uniform he and other members wear to march in an annual parade. *Sheila Bailey*.

The Merci Boxcar contains memorabilia from the Second World War. *Sheila Bailey.*

The black boxcar is decorated with colorful shields, each representing a province in France. Travia helps visitors up the steep step to the boxcar and shows off the treasures inside. He knows the provenance of each scrap of paper and each tarnished medal.

While the priest's land is secure for now, the spot off Bremer Street, on Manchester's West Side, is hard to find and even harder to park at. Travia has been negotiating with the New Hampshire Veterans Cemetery in Boscawen for a possible spot there. There would be a lot more exposure there, and he envisions a viewing room with a short DVD about the boxcar.

He's eager to see such an important piece of history be preserved and seen.[102]

A Father's Promise: The State Marine Memorial, Hampton Beach

In the beginning, William Downs just wanted to remember his son.[103]

Downs, a resident of Manchester, lost his son Captain William D. Downs in the Pacific theater during World War II. The younger Downs was buried at sea on May 25, 1945. His father sought help from the federal government for a memorial—a token gravesite—but was rejected. Downs then tried to establish a memorial in the nation's capital to all who were lost at sea, but his efforts proved fruitless.

But Downs struck gold closer to home. In 1950, he approached then-governor Sherman Adams about a state memorial to his son and the thousands of others lost at sea. Adams created the New Hampshire Marine Memorial Commission, and the group began to search for a site.

The commission explored other sites in Rye and Rye Harbor before settling on the Hampton Beach parcel across from the Ashworth Hotel. Funds were raised, land was leveled and a design was sought. The winning design came from Concord artist Alice Cosgrove. She was already working for her fellow New Hampshire citizens as the state commercial artist, designing ski brochures and creating "Chippa Granite," the freckle-faced boy child who represented the state for most of the 1950s. Chippa, best described as Beaver Cleaver on skis, faded into kitsch, but the marine memorial lives on.

Cosgrove made a scale model of her design. A Cambridge, Massachusetts sculptor, Teodors Usarins, made a life-sized model in clay, working closely with Cosgrove to reproduce the face and feeling in her design. The statue was made of local granite that was quarried at the Swenson Granite Company in Concord. It was shipped to Vermont for shaping by Italian sculptor Vincenzo Andreani. Andreani used a plaster cast of *The Lady* for measurements. The cast is now kept in the Tuck Museum in Hampton.

The statue has a six-foot-tall base and rises to a height of twelve feet. The granite bench is twenty feet long and two feet, six inches wide and four feet tall. Its ten columns bear the original 248 names, with an inscription, "In memorial of New Hampshire's war dead lost at sea in defense of our country."

Captain William D. Downs was the inspiration for the *Marine Memorial* at Hampton Beach. *Hampton Historical Society.*

TYPICAL CHIPPA on skis represents New Hampshire on posters and folders promoting Granite State winter sports everywhere.

Chippa Granite was the creation of Alice Cosgrove, a staff artist with the State of New Hampshire, who also created the design for the *Marine Memorial* at Hampton Beach. *Hampton Historical Society.*

Sculptor Vincenzo Andreoni is shown working on the *Marine Memorial*, a New Hampshire monument to all who are lost at sea. *Hampton Historical Society.*

Dignitaries assemble to dedicate the *New Hampshire Marine Memorial* in May 1957. Kathleen Kelly Mullen of Concord (*left*), the founder of the New Hampshire Gold Star Mothers, waits to unveil the statue, which was presented by Governor Lane Dwinnell. At the podium is Reverend Daniel Poling of Deering, whose son was one of the "Four Chaplains" who died at sea after giving their life vests to four other soldiers. *Hampton Historical Society.*

Above: The state Marine Memorial was dedicated on May 30, 1957. It was the brainchild of Granite Stater William Downs. *Hampton Historical Society.*

Left: "Breathe soft, ye winds, ye waves in silence sleep / Let prosp'rous breezes wanton o'er the deep / Swell the white sails, and with the streamers play / To waft her gently o'er the watry way." John Gay, "Epistle to a Lady." The poem is inscribed on the Marine Memorial. *Sheila Bailey.*

The New Hampshire Marine Memorial was dedicated on May 30, 1957. "The Lady" continues to preside over Hampton Beach, with her gaze fixed on the unpredictable, uncontrollable ocean. At the base of the statue, the words from John Gay's poem "An Epistle to a Lady" are carved at Cosgrove's suggestion. "Breathe soft, ye winds, ye waves in silence rest." While the statue is located in Hampton Beach, it speaks for all of New Hampshire and every branch of service.

ALBACORE MEMORIAL GARDEN

The USS *Albacore* is a research submarine that is open to the public at Albacore Park in Portsmouth. The grounds include a memorial garden with monuments to those lost in various submarine disasters.

HOW WE LIVED: THE WRIGHT MUSEUM

The late David Wright opened the Wright Museum in Wolfeboro in 1994 to honor the contributions of Americans to winning the Second World War. Wright built the museum around his collection of antique military vehicles, but it soon became much more. From the home front to the battlefield, the military's exploits are celebrated in dioramas, displays, timelines and life-sized replicas of the rooms and stores of the 1940s.

Visitors enter through a lobby of rotating exhibits. At the time of this book's publication, the exhibit displayed posters of the Norman Rockwell Four Freedoms series: *Freedom of Speech*, with a man standing up in the town meeting so dear to New Hampshire; *Freedom of Worship*; *Freedom from Want*, with the iconic grandmother serving the turkey; and *Freedom from Fear*. Franklin D. Roosevelt's "Four Freedoms" speech plays a haunting accompaniment in the background.

Life-sized dioramas show the home front, with a soda fountain, gas station and the perennial five-and-dime. The dioramas morph into scenes of life in wartime, with a small child in a replica uniform and a large console radio waiting to dispense the next "Fireside Chat." There's an homage to the victory garden, housewives saving cooking oil, children corralling every bit of scrap metal. It was an effort never seen in the country before and not replicated since, and the Wright makes the most of every scrap of rubber.

The *Albacore* submarine in Portsmouth features a memorial garden to honor those who lost their lives in submarines. *Sheila Bailey.*

This replica of an army barracks is part of the life-sized displays at the Wright Museum, a Wolfeboro museum devoted to the battle and home fronts of the Second World War. *Sheila Bailey.*

A WAAC (Women's Army Auxiliary Corps) uniform is part of the exhibits at the Wright Museum in Wolfeboro. *Sheila Bailey.*

The late David Wright's collection of military vehicles led to the establishment of a museum bearing his name that is dedicated to the efforts of Americans in the Second World War. *Sheila Bailey.*

A series of walk-through rooms takes visitors through the war years from Hitler's invasion of Poland in 1939 to the triumph of VE and VJ Days. Period music plays along with clips from popular movies and morale-boosting newsreels. The theme continues with a mezzanine floor, in which the Wright pays tribute to every branch of the service, with a special focus on women and their contributions.

The museum boasts fourteen thousand items from the period, in addition to operational vehicles and airplanes. The Wright Museum has frequent public programs and special exhibitions, all targeted toward explaining why the Greatest Generation was so great.[104]

No Sacrifice Unnoted: The Veterans Cemetery

The New Hampshire State Veterans Cemetery was established on July 1, 1997, in a move by both the state and federal governments. It took over 104 acres of forested land in Boscawen. Phase one construction on 9 acres was completed in November 1997. The current facility covers 14

The New Hampshire Veterans' Cemetery, Boscawen. *Sheila Bailey.*

The many faces of the U.S. Army over the years are shown in this installation at the New Hampshire Veterans' Cemetery, Boscawen. *Sheila Bailey.*

acres and includes a carillon system, a memorial brick walkway, a Circle of Flags and monuments to various branches of the service and historic military endeavors.

The first interment there was that of U.S. Navy veteran Chief Warrant Officer 2 Ernest Holm (World War I and World War II) on November 18, 1997, alongside his wife, Hilda. The New Hampshire Veterans Cemetery was the first military cemetery east of the Mississippi that allowed loved ones to be buried with their veterans.

The Veterans Cemetery is inclusive, honoring the war dead from every branch, every gender—and every race. In November 2010, more than one hundred Natives and their supporters gathered at the cemetery for the unveiling of a monument honoring Natives who served their country at war. The monument, funded by the New Hampshire Intertribal Native American Council, is in the shape of a drum covered by an arch and reads, "Dedicated to all Native American Veterans / American and Canadian / Who served to protect / This land called / Turtle Island." The cemetery also contains a monument to Catholic war veterans.[105]

This monument honors the Natives who fought in the country's various conflicts. *Sheila Bailey*.

Catholic war veterans are honored with this monument at the New Hampshire Veterans' Cemetery, Boscawen. *Sheila Bailey*.

THE WAR DOGS MEMORIAL, BARRINGTON

The War Dogs Memorial was dedicated in 2002 by American Legion Post 114 of Barrington and is located in Pine Grove Cemetery on Route 9 near the historical society. It was sculpted by Stephen Roy, and the inscription reads, "In memory of those war dogs who were truly man's best friend."

Since World War I, thousands of dogs have been deployed with their handlers, and thousands have died on the field of battle. *Always Faithful*, a life-sized statue of a Doberman Pinscher, can be found on the island of Guam and represents twenty-five dogs that died helping Marines liberate Guam in 1944. A replica of the statue is at the Marine Corps Research Center in Quantico, Virginia.

The largest deployment of military working dogs served during the Vietnam War, with five thousand dogs and ten thousand handlers deployed over four branches of the military. They were used for walking point, tracking and sniffing out mines.[106]

This monument in Barrington's cemetery honors the dogs who helped America win its wars. *Joy Leclair, Living with a Golden website.*

Remembrance, Squared

When Manchester ran out of room for monuments, it began naming squares and small parks for its war heroes. In addition to the William Jutras Square (chapter 3) and Roger Cote Square (chapter 5), it boasts squares dedicated to the following.[107]

- Arthur St. Pierre, 1920–1944
- Bernard B. Barry, 1893–1918
- Bernard C. Mullen, 1908–1944
- Francis P. Lally, 1919–1943
- Gerald R. Helmich, 1931–1969
- Herman F. Little, 1893–1918
- J. Roger Raymond, 1921–1943
- John J. Sullivan, 1907–1942
- Joseph H. W. Roux, 1921–1943
- Maurice St. Germain, 1921–1941
- Robert W. Lewis, 1922–1942
- Roland A. Metivier, 1919–1943

The Men Behind the Chisels

Many noted artists turned their talents to honoring those who gave their all.

The Sculptors: Lucien Gosselin

Lucien Hippolyte Gosselin spent his career serving the town and community he loved.

The French Canadian sculptor's work dots his adopted city of Manchester, New Hampshire, where he taught at the former New Hampshire Institute of Art. His works tell the story of a place, a time and a people.

Gosselin was born in Whitefield, New Hampshire, to emigrants from Quebec, but he moved to Manchester at the age of two and claimed the city as his home. He worked with his brothers in a barbershop but began studying art with Manchester artist Emile Maupas. Maupas and Bishop George Guertin encouraged him to study in Paris, and he did so at the Academie

Julian beginning in 1911. His work attracted attention in Paris, and he won several awards. He escaped the war, returning to America in 1916, but the war informed his work and his commissions for the rest of his life.

Gosselin is responsible for the florid, emotional monument at the center of Manchester's Victory Park. The memorial pulls out every stop, including an allegorical mourning figure, Columbia, a soldier, a sailor and eagles.

He was also commissioned to create the bust of Henry J. Sweeney, the first Manchester man to die in the Great War. And in 1939, he honored his own people with a monument in Mount Calvary Cemetery honoring the French Canadians who served in the war.

Gosselin ventured out of the state for special projects, such as the World War I memorial honoring parishioners of Notre Dame de Lourdes Church in Fall River, Massachusetts, who gave their lives in the conflict. Twenty-two parishioners were killed in that war. The monument features a replica of the Sacred Heart overlooking an angel and a dying soldier. He also created the Dubois Memorial in Laconia, the Monsignor Millette Memorial in Nashua, the Father Boissoneault Memorial in St. Johnsbury, Vermont, and the Gatineau Monument in Southbridge, Massachusetts.

He is also responsible for a series of carved figures inside St. Joseph Cathedral and was the sculptor of the statue of Casimir Pulaski on horseback in Pulaski Park in Manchester.

Though Gosselin received international acclaim and honors, he never forgot Manchester, because he never left. He was buried in Mount Calvary Cemetery, among the French Canadians he loved and celebrated.[108]

The Sculptors: Martin Milmore

Milmore emigrated from Ireland at the age of seven and settled in Boston during the "no Irish need apply" years. Because his family was Protestant, he avoided most of the country's anti-Irish sentiment. He attended Boston Latin School, graduating in 1860. He studied with the prominent sculptor Thomas Ball, and when Ball moved to Italy, Milmore and his brother Joseph, a stonecutter, opened their own studio.

Milmore was soon in demand to create memorials, particularly those commemorating the losses of a long and brutal war. His work can be seen in at least four New Hampshire towns.

The townspeople of Amherst commissioned Milmore to create their statue after the War Between the States. The casting was done by Ames

Manufacturing Co. of Chicopee, Massachusetts. His other three works in New Hampshire may be found in Claremont, Peterborough and Keene.

He was also the sculptor for the Soldiers and Sailors Monument on the Boston Common. The City of Boston allotted $75,000 for the monument. The monument is seventy feet tall with a sixteen-foot-tall stone pedestal. A bronze statue of a woman signifies the Genius of America on top of a white marble Doric column. The four projecting pedestals have figures representing the north, south, east and west, and at the base of the column, four more statues represent the Soldier, the Sailor, History and Peace. Bronze reliefs depict other scenes from the War Between the States. The installation is a veritable history of Massachusetts in the war.

But another story is told in the sorrowful, brooding "Single Soldiers" Milmore produced for New Hampshire's small towns.

Milmore's talent blazed brightly before his death at the age of thirty-nine. He earned the recognition of his peers, including Daniel Chester French, who designed Milmore's own monument in Forest Hills Cemetery in Jamaica Plain, Massachusetts.[109]

The Sculptors: Daniel Chester French

Daniel Chester French left Exeter as a teen but never forgot his hometown. He designed the World War I sculpture at Gale Park in Exeter. Alice Gale Hobson donated the land in memory of her father, General Stephen H. Gale. The park and memorial were dedicated on July 4, 1922.[110]

While French is famous for the *Minuteman* statue and the Lincoln Memorial, his work can also be seen in New Hampshire. He designed *Death and Youth*, the World War I memorial in the Chapel of Saint Peter and Saint Paul at Saint Paul's School in Concord. The sculpture is of an angel holding a young dying soldier. The sculpture is in an alcove, and the wall bears the names of the forty-eight Saint Paul's School graduates who gave their lives in the war.[111]

French also designed the statue of Commodore George Hamilton Perkins at the statehouse.[112] Henry Bacon was the architect, and the statue was erected in 1902. French also designed the pediment over the main door of the New Hampshire Historical Society on Park Street in Concord.

The Sculptors: Leonard Craske

Leonard Craske is remembered most for his sculpture of the *Gloucester Fisherman* at the entrance to the Stacy Esplanade in Gloucester, Massachusetts. The statue, also known as the *Man at the Wheel*, was commissioned by the Gloucester Tercentenary Permanent Memorial Association. The association wanted to commemorate the town's three hundredth anniversary and permanently memorialize the fishermen lost at sea.

Craske made the design. The cast was made by the Gorham Company of Providence, Rhode Island, and the statue was unveiled in 1925. The cost was $10,000. The statue is similar to New Hampshire's marine memorial in that the names of those lost at sea—in Gloucester's case, three thousand—are engraved at the base of the monument. The memorial also includes the names of the captain and crew of the *Andrea Gail*, who were lost at sea in 1991 and were the basis for the book and movie *The Perfect Storm*.

The Gloucester statue was added to the National Register of Historic Places in 1936.

The model for the statue was Gloucester fisherman Captain Clayton Morrissey. Ironically, he died at sea in 1936 on his trawler *Nimbus* due to a heart attack.

Craske was born in England in 1882 and lived until 1950. He had several careers, including studying medicine in London. But his need to paint and draw was too strong, and he took courses after dropping out of medical school. He worked as an actor in England, and afterward, he moved to Boston before he put his anatomical training to work as a sculptor. His *Gloucester Fisherman* won the competition for the three hundredth anniversary, and for several years, he was busy with commission work.

Craske also designed the *Doughboy* statue in Amesbury, Massachusetts, that was unveiled on November 11, 1929.

The demand for Craske's sculptures dried up during the Depression and in World War II, when the government commandeered bronze for weapons. Undaunted, Craske invented himself again, capitalizing on an interest in photography to experiment with color and special effects. He lectured in photography and judged competitions in the Boston area. He liked photography because it gave him a chance to work with color.

But Craske never lost his love for three-dimensional work, and he began working on a statue to memorialize those lost in the First World War, with a suffering Christ looking down on a dying soldier. The model for the piece, *Ecce Homo*, is kept at the museum at the Cathedral of the Pines and is a lasting tribute to his talent and those who served.[113]

The Sculptors: Augustus Saint-Gaudens

Augustus Saint-Gaudens distinguished himself as a sculptor. While he was not a New Hampshire native, much of his work lives on in the Saint-Gaudens National Historic Site on the grounds of his former summer home in Cornish. He was raised in New York City and studied in Europe. His work ranged from classical pieces, such as his *Diana* at Madison Square Garden, to designing coins, including the double eagle gold piece in 1907. He founded the Cornish Colony, where noted artists, such as Harry Thrasher, studied.[114]

Saint-Gaudens was to earn at least part of his reputation through designing and constructing war memorials. He produced the General John Logan Memorial in Chicago's Grant Park, the William Tecumseh Sherman statue in New York's Central Park and the Admiral Farragut statue at Madison Square Park, a copy of which can be seen in Cornish. He memorialized President Lincoln at least twice, with his *Abraham Lincoln: The Man* at Lincoln Park in Chicago and a seated Lincoln, *Abraham Lincoln, the Head of State*, in Chicago's Grant Park.

The bronze bas-relief basis for Saint-Gaudens's Robert Gould Shaw Memorial is considered one of his greatest works. He labored on it for fourteen years, with the first public version unveiled on the Boston Common in 1897. Another version can be seen at the historic site. Among other things, the Robert Gould Shaw Memorial is noted for its realistic depiction of Black soldiers trudging along behind their commander. Each one is a different, fully realized portrait on its own, giving the North a fuller vision of what it fought for.[115]

Diagnosed with cancer in 1900, Saint-Gaudens spent the rest of his life at the Cornish property, working and teaching other artists until his death in 1907.[116]

The Last Word

$\mathcal{J}$im Pope wants to make one thing clear: he isn't anti-statue, or anti-obelisk, or anti-plaque.

But he isn't sure they're doing the job.

Pope speaks with an easy drawl reminiscent of the late Jimmy Stewart, a man whose onscreen and offscreen ideals mirror Pope's. Pope did his bit to help his country, but unlike Stewart, he did it in the least popular war in the nation's history. He did three deployments to Vietnam, each for about nine months, between 1962 and 1967, and it colored the way he looks at war, heroes and the way we remember them.

Pope, a member of the Kilduff-Wirtanen American Legion Post, was recently involved in conversations about how the town could remember those who died in the War on Terror. He remembers looking around at the monuments the town already has, mostly clustered in the town hall area, and thinking, "Memorials are looking backward. They are tributes to past events, set up after the end."

His views were honed by looking at and thinking about the memorials to those who served in Vietnam, the two Iraq Wars and Afghanistan. "They do not work," he said of the monuments. "We keep making all the same mistakes." But at the time of this book's publication, Pope pointed out, "There is no end in sight for the War on Terror." While previous wars were specific, time-limited events, the War on Terror is still going on in numerous

This model of the proposed *Pillars of Freedom* monument will point Americans toward a solution to war, rather than looking back. *Jim Pope.*

venues around the world. "I didn't want a 'memorial' to the war but to what it's fighting for," Pope said.

Pope and others brainstormed and came up with the *Pillars of Freedom*. "We talk about the things we want to do," Pope said. "We want to see peace; we want to see freedom; we want to pass democracy along. What helps us to do this? Not reflecting on past deeds but passing on ideals."

The legion formed a committee and found a sculptor, John Weidman, from the faculty of the nearby Andres Institute. They worked with him on a design, which will be a six-sided pillar listing the freedoms they want to safeguard. They're currently raising funds, with a goal of $34,000.

Pillars of Freedom is a granite monument composed of a base and hexagonal column topped with a sphere. The column is five feet, two inches tall and two feet in diameter. The sphere, also granite, is two feet in diameter. The granite base will be four feet square and four inches thick, with a walkway of engraved bricks.

The pillars the monument will uphold were adapted from the American Legion's constitution and include the following:

- To inculcate a sense of individual obligation to community, state and nation;
- To combat the autocracy of both the classes and the masses;
- To make right the master of might;
- To promote peace and goodwill on earth;
- To safeguard and transmit to posterity the principles of justice, freedom and democracy; and
- To uphold and defend the Constitution of the United States of America.

The monument will also depict the insignias of the service branches of the United States, including the Army, Marines, Air Force, Navy, Space Force and Coast Guard, in bronze.

As for Pope, he'll continue to raise funds and fight for freedom through the age-old medium of art. "With the wars that go on forever, it's a group effort," he explained. "It's bigger than one person."

Notes

Chapter 1

1. *Exterior Memorials and Other Structures at the New Hampshire State House* (Relay: New Hampshire Division of Cultural Resources, n.d.), n.p.
2. George Morrison, phone interviews with author, 2021.
3. Kieran O'Keefe, "Monuments to the American Revolution," *Journal of the American Revolution*, September 17, 2019.
4. See chapter 3 and the appendix.
5. See page 23 (John Stark).
6. Ibid.
7. Ibid.
8. Ibid.
9. Ibid.
10. Ibid.
11. Ibid.
12. Ibid.
13. Ibid.

Chapter 2

14. Morrison interviews, 2021.
15. JoAnn Tebbetts, phone interviews with the author, 2021.

16. New Hampshire Veterans Association, "Timeline," www.weisbeach.com.

17. Castle Freeman, "The 'Single Soldier' Monument," *Yankee*, May 2015.

18. Cara Giamo, "These Mass-Produced Civil War Statues Were Made to Stand Forever," Atlas Obscura, August 25, 2017.

19. WTTW Chicago Public Radio, "10 Monuments that Changed America," www.wttw.com.

20. See the appendix.

21. See page 56 ("Single Soldiers").

22. Ibid.

23. Ibid.

24. See the appendix.

25. See page 55 (Robert Shaw Memorial).

26. See the appendix.

27. See page 53 (Manchester).

28. Ibid.

29. Ibid.

30. Ibid.

31. Ibid.

32. See the introduction.

33. Ibid.

34. See page 48 (Loammi Bean Fountain).

35. Ibid.

36. Ibid.

Chapter 3

37. City of Manchester website, www.manchesternh.gov.

38. Ibid.

39. See the appendix.

40. New Hampshire Historical Society, "Marlow," www.nhhistory.org.

41. See chapter 8.

42. Atkinson Historical Society, www.atkinsonhistoricalsociety.org.

43. See page 78 (Berlin); Paul Tardiff, "Once Upon a Berlin Time," March 2003.

44. Center Harbor Artillery Relief Sculpture, Smithsonian American Art Museum, Renwick Gallery, www.washington.org/smithsonian.

45. See the appendix.

46. See chapter 3 and the appendix.

47. Hampton Historical Society, Lane Library, www.hampton.lib.us.
48. Hooksett Historical Society. www.hooksett.org/historicalsociety.
49. See the introduction (page 79) and (page 81).
50. See page 80 (Manchester).
51. Jutras Post, American Legion, Manchester, jutraspost43nh.com.
52. Hillsborough County Genealogy, compiled by Helen Coughlin, www. genealogytrails.com.
53. Ibid.
54. Ibid.
55. Ibid.
56. Larry Cote, Newport Historical Society, newportnhhistory.org.
57. See page 86 (Harry Thrasher).
58. Ibid.
59. See pages 89 and 8.

Chapter 4

60. Shawne K. Wickham, "Flag Raising Wasn't What Made Rene Gagnon a Hero," *New Hampshire Union Leader*, October 21, 2019.
61. Ibid.
62. See chapter 2.
63. General Thyng obituary, *New York Times*, September 27, 1983.
64. See page 118.
65. Ibid.; New England Ski Museum, newenglandskimuseum.org; Roberts Armory, a Traveling World War II Museum, www.robertsarmory.com.
66. New Hampshire Division of Historical Resources, "New Hampshire Historical Markers," www.NH.gov.
67. Hooksett Historical Society, www.hooksett.org/historicalsociety.
68. See page 115 (Manchester).
69. Ibid.
70. See the appendix.
71. See chapter 4, page 115 (Manchester).
72. See chapter 2.
73. Hillsborough County Genealogy.
74. Ibid.
75. Courtesy of the Milford Historical Society, www.milfordhistory.com.
76. Larry Cote, Newport Historical Society, www.newporthistory.org.
77. See page 120 (Harrison Thyng).

78. Ibid.
79. See chapter 8.

Chapter 5

80. Hillsborough County Genealogy.
81. See page 142 (Berlin).
82. Ibid.
83. Ibid.

Chapter 6

84. U.S. Department of Veterans Affairs, Office of Research and Development, "National Vietnam Veterans Research Study," 1983, www.va.gov.
85. Gina Harkins, October 2019, www.military.com.
86. See chapter 8.
87. Hillsborough County Genealogy.
88. Ibid.
89. Shawne K. Wickham, "50 Years Later, Manchester Remembers 'The Saddest Day,'" *New Hampshire Union Leader*, August 24, 2019.
90. *New Hampshire Sunday News*, August 31, 1969.
91. Ibid.
92. See page 155.
93. Ibid.
94. Ibid.
95. Ibid.
96. Ibid.

Chapter 7

97. See page 171.
98. Ibid.
99. Ibid.
100. Ibid.
101. Ibid.

Appendix

102. For more information or a tour, contact Travia at travia11@comcast.net.
103. John Holman from the Hampton Historical Society.
104. 77 Center Street, Wolfeboro, NH; 603-569-1212; visit www.wrightmuseum.org.
105. 110 Daniel Webster Highway, Boscawen, NH; 603-796-2026.
106. For more information, visit the Vietnam Dog Handlers Association at www.vdha.us.
107. Hillsborough County Genealogy; City of Manchester website, www.manchester.nh.gov.
108. See chapters 1 and 3.
109. See chapter 2.
110. See chapter 3.
111. See "Listings: World War I."
112. See chapter 2.
113. See chapters 3 and 8.
114. See chapter 3.
115. See chapter 2.
116. Route 12A, Cornish, NH; 603-675-2175.

About the Authors

Kathleen Bailey is a journalist and novelist with forty years' experience in the nonfiction, newspaper and inspirational fields. Born in 1951, she was a child in the '50s, a teen in the '60s, a young adult in the '70s and a young mom in the '80s. It's been a turbulent, colorful time to grow up, and she's enjoyed every minute of it—and written about most of it. While she's always dreamed of publishing fiction and has three novels in print, her two Arcadia projects, *Past and Present Exeter* and *New Hampshire War Monuments*, made her fall in love with nonfiction and telling real people's stories. She lives in Raymond, New Hampshire.

Sheila Bailey is a freelance photographer living in Concord, New Hampshire. She enjoys traveling around her state and New England looking for the perfect shot. She recently coauthored *Past and Present Exeter*, along with shooting the contemporary photographs for *War Monuments*.

Visit us at
www.historypress.com
··